CLAIM YOUR FREE 30 SECOND PRESENTATION MASTER

Simply complete this coupon and send it to us to receive your free guide to perfect presentation. Packed with tips and practical suggestions the 30 SECOND PRESENTATION MASTER helps you make first-class presentations every time.

☐ *I would like to receive further information on the Ready Made Activities Resource Packs*

Name: _____ Position: _____

Company/Organisation: _____

Address (including postcode): _____

_____

Country: _____

Telephone: _____ Fax: _____

Nature of business: _____

Title of book purchased: _____

Comments: _____

_____

-------------------------------- | **Fold Here Then Staple** | --------------------------------

We would be very grateful if you could answer these questions to help us with market research.

1 Where/How did you hear of this book?
☐ in a bookshop
☐ in a magazine/newspaper
(please state which):

_____

☐ information through the post
☐ recommendation from a colleague
☐ other (please state which):

2 Which newspaper(s)/magazine(s) do you read regularly?:

_____

_____

_____

3 When buying a business book which factors influence you most?
(Please rank in order)
☐ recommendation from a colleague
☐ price
☐ content
☐ recommendation in a books⊦
☐ author
☐ publisher
☐ title
☐ other(s):

_____

4 Is this book a
☐ personal purchase?
☐ company purchase?

5 Would you be prepared to spend a few minutes talking to our customer services staff to help with product development? YES/NO

Claim your 30 Second Presentation Master
FREE *from Pitman Publishing*

Simply complete the reverse of this coupon and send it to us – no stamp needed –
to claim your FREE 30 SECOND PRESENTATION MASTER – packed with tips
and practical suggestions to help make a first-class presentation every time.

Ready Made Activities Resource Packs

The really practical way to run YOUR coaching session. Each Resource Pack
contains all the information you can find in the paperback Ready Made
Activities... books, plus much, much more!

- **Free Video**
  Use it to introduce the session or reinforce your message
- **Overhead Transparencies**
  Studio designed for a professional presentation – no fuss, no poor handwriting,
  no spelling mistakes!
- **Photocopiable Handouts**
  Summaries of all the main points for your group to take away.
  No need to write notes, accuracy guaranteed.

Plus

- **£100 OFF WHEN YOU PURCHASE A SELECTED VIDEO FROM
  LONGMAN TRAINING!**

Tick the box overleaf for more information on the Ready Made Activities Resource Packs

----

Free Information Service
Pitman Professional Publishing
FREEPOST
128 Long Acre
LONDON
WC2E 9BR, UK

No stamp
necessary
in the UK

Ready made activities for
DEVELOPING YOUR STAFF

IMI *information service*
Sandyford, Dublin 16
Telephone 2078513 Fax 295 9479
email library@imi.ie
Internet http://www.imi.ie

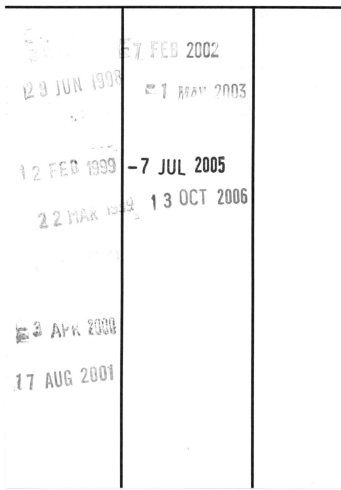

Ready made activities for DEVELOPING YOUR STAFF

Sue Bishop

David Taylor

the Institute
of Management

FOUNDATION

PITMAN
PUBLISHING

PITMAN PUBLISHING
128 Long Acre, London WC2E 9AN

A Division of Longman Group UK Limited

First published in Great Britain 1994

© Sue Bishop and David Taylor, 1994

British Library Cataloguing in Publication Data
A CIP catalogue record for this book can be obtained from the British Library.

ISBN 0 273 60560 7

10 9 8 7 6 5 4 3 2 1

Typeset by PanTek Arts, Maidstone, Kent.
Printed and bound in Great Britain by Clays Ltd, St Ives plc.

The Publishers' policy is to use paper manufactured from sustainable forests.

Contents

Preface

The book is intended to enable those with responsibility for the delivery of training to produce top quality events for participants on their courses. Part One of the book gives a detailed guide to facilitation – how to deliver 'quality training'. Part Two is a much longer section containing training activities. These are intended primarily for use by managers/supervisors with their own staff, and are focused on helping individuals and work teams to deliver high quality service to internal and external customers – if you will, 'training in quality'.

WHO THIS BOOK IS FOR

Although of use to professional facilitators, this book is targeted more at a new generation of trainers: line managers and supervisors whose expanded responsibilities now involve up-front training. Not only are businesses finding it increasingly difficult to resource centralised training sections, along with specialist trainers, but many learning events are better done at departmental or section level. It's no use training the managers only of course – total quality requires a commitment from everyone, from the managing director to the person who replaces the light bulbs.

Many businesses are already creating pools of 'temporary trainers' from within, and it is primarily for such people that this book has been written.

All managers and supervisors are trainers, of course, by definition. Most, though, would see the training they do as mainly one-to-one coaching or mentoring. We are tackling, in this book,'group' training events. Some managers and supervisors will feel themselves ill-equipped to carry out this role; they may feel lacking in skills and/or confidence to carry it out effectively. Others may relish the challenge but feel they lack suitable material around which to build training events.

This book is for both groups. It's aimed at managers and supervisors who are committed to being in the front line of training delivery for their own staff.

USING THE MATERIAL IN THIS BOOK

There is a pretty hefty assumption built into this book: the activities will be used mainly by managers and supervisors with their own teams; probably groups that have been set up as Quality Action Teams. These are defined by Tony Newby as:

> small groups of (usually) lower-level employees who meet regularly and work within a structured framework to identify and resolve problems that affect their ability to deliver the best possible quality of service.
>
> (Newby, 1992: p.20)

It is primarily for use with such groups that our book has been written. Manager/trainers will thus already know something about their participants. This has its benefits, but there is a 'downside' too. We talk about this in Part One.

There is another big assumption which we have made: large chunks of time will not be available for training events. We have therefore not devised structured training courses but training activities. These can stand alone perfectly well or they can be integrated into broader training events. For the most part they are short and can be easily fitted into an extended lunchtime, a late afternoon – or even breakfast? – session.

This book hasn't been written to try and turn people into scintillating trainers overnight. We do, though, try to provide some thoughts within the activities as to how you might process each one. This requires skill and practice. We supply some ideas on the skills but only you can do the practice!

THE BOOK'S STRUCTURE

The book is divided into two major parts in addition to this Preface.

Part 1 Facilitating group learning events

This will take you through the basics of effective training practice, with the emphasis firmly (if not 100 per cent exclusively) on **facilitating** rather than lecturing. You will be given practical, down-to-earth ideas about how to ensure your training events are relevant and effective and – equally important – seen as such by those undergoing them. Even if you feel you know the ropes, you may yet find some new perspectives in this section.

We do ask everyone to find time to read through Part One. It's been written in (we hope) a non-theoretical way with the emphasis on **doing**. For those who want to pursue the theory, we have suggested some further reading and references in a short Bibliography.

There's nothing radically new in Part One. Experienced facilitators will be familiar with the ideas – but that's just the point! We **know** the ideas work and so we focus on tried and tested techniques. Between us we have many years experience of group training and facilitation. We both believe that the best learning takes place when people are actively involved in the learning process rather than as passive participants. We offer some of the best ideas on how to create an effective learning environment, not only during the event itself but also before and after.

Part 2 Activities

The Activities in Part Two all provide some measure of active involvement as an intrinsic part of their design. They are intended to extend individuals' skills, to develop teamwork, and improve quality service and customer care. Some of the Activities offer training in baseline skills, and are therefore basic, simple and straightforward. Others are more developmental. There is a small number which could be used by managers who have other managers or supervisors in their team. There is one fairly risky one which inexperienced managers may prefer to leave alone! There is also one Activity which consists of a possible (different) approach to managing a group learning event, rather than being a clear-cut activity in its own right. You will find a variety of approaches, including small-group work, competitive 'games', role plays, case studies, questionnaires and so on.

Some Activities are seemingly light-hearted (though not lightweight; they have a serious purpose!) **All** have clear learning benefits if delivered properly. The benefits are described in each activity's Aim.

Each Activity is structured in the same way, offering:

- description of the activity
- its aim (or benefits)
- time required
- list of resources needed to run it
- method to be followed.

The Method is a step-by-step guide to running the Activity. It outlines procedures to be followed, gives time guidance where necessary and offers ideas on how to ensure that participants actually learn something!

Broad principles of group facilitation are not repeated in every activity but are contained in Part One, so please ensure you read that FIRST, before embarking on any of the activities with your own team.

The guidance notes within each Activity are specific to that Activity. Essentially they consist of :

- what to do and when
- questions you might use to get relevant discussion going
- some pitfalls to avoid (when relevant)
- Exercises, Handouts and Trainer notes, any or all of which may be freely copied or photocopied for use during the Activity.

THE BOOK'S FOCUS

The Activities are designed to develop individuals and teams so that they might better understand and deliver quality service through superior customer care. There are, of course, many different aspects to customer care and quality and you will find activities which cover all the common ones. There are others which are more peripheral. Although customers and quality are central to the thinking behind the activities, we deliberately do not define either too tightly, so if you find an Activity that you feel you would like to use in another context then please feel free to do so!

Most of the Activities are brand new, although a small number represent adaptations of tried and tested activities which the authors have used and whose origins are lost in the mist of time. Please use and adapt these Activities to meet your own or your team's particular needs; we definitely want to encourage flexibility. There are no 'tablets of stone' qualities to our Activities.

The Activities appear in the book in the following order:

- basic communication skills (5 activities)
- assertion skills (4 activities)
- teamwork (8 activities)
- perceptions (6 activities)
- quality standards (4 activities)
- the learning event (3 activities)

More detailed information is contained within each activity itself.

CONCLUSION

We do hope that you will find the book useful, whether you are an experienced manager/trainer looking for new material on quality or customer care or whether you are one of the growing legions of 'temporary trainers' anxious about taking on the role of group facilitator for the first time. We both came into training by way of our managerial roles and we have never regretted it. We would, in our early days of experimenting with different training techniques, have loved a book like this – which is why we have written it! Have fun – why shouldn't you?

As is usual with our jointly written books we would like to set on record our real appreciation of the support and understanding of Mags, Val and Niel during the period when we were developing and writing the material.

Sue Bishop
David Taylor
April 1994

1

....

FACILITATING GROUP LEARNING EVENTS

1 Introduction

So why should I spend valuable time reading this long chapter on facilitation?
If you're already an experienced trainer who knows the difference between group training and group facilitation, you don't need to. Skip it.
But if you're:

- a 'temporary trainer' who has been enlisted (willingly, we hope) to help out with training your colleagues, or
- a trainer more used to presenting, lecturing or what is often called the 'chalk and talk' approach, or
- a trainer new to facilitation and who would benefit from additional guidance, or
- a manager/supervisor/team leader who is anxious at the thought of running group learning/development events

then this chapter really is a must.

(A brief word on semantics is needed here. Since the book is designed to be used by the range of people suggested above, we have decided to adopt a convention throughout this book. When we talk about a 'trainer' we are referring to someone who has a responsibility to train others. When we talk about a 'facilitator' we mean someone who is adopting the principles in this book in order to create a good learning experience. When we talk about a 'manager' we are thinking of anyone who has some kind of managerial responsibility, be it as manager, supervisor, team leader and so on.)

The Activities in Part Two provide plenty of help and ideas on how to 'process' an activity *but they all assume a basic grasp of what group facilitation is about.*

Facilitating a group training event can be very rewarding, but the initial sense of 'letting go' – of letting them get on with it – can make you feel very vulnerable, powerless, as if you're losing control . . . all very familiar feelings to anyone who tries facilitation for the first few times . . . and all quite normal. If you can make a go of it though, you will never look back, and nor will your participants.

This is not to say that there isn't a place for the more traditional approach – lecturing, telling, informing, briefing, presenting – of course there is, but the Activities in this book are not about these techniques.

This book is designed to take you on a journey. The destination is, in itself, just a beginning. Our hope is that, once you have read Part One, thought about it, acted on it and used some of the Activities from Part Two, you will have 'arrived' at the point where you (consciously) and your participants (unconsciously) will have begun to appreciate the significant learning benefits of good facilitation. To pursue this analogy of the journey, we have set down a number of 'Landmarks' on the way. These appear at the ends of Chapters 2, 3 and 5 and in the middle of Chapter 4. We refer to them as Landmarks since their purpose is to enable you to monitor your own progress. Taken together, and in sequence, the Landmarks offer you a guide to that rewarding journey; organising, setting up, facilitating and evaluating a successful learning event.

What follows is divided up into four main areas:

- Training Needs Analysis
- From training needs to learning objectives
- The skills of facilitation
- Evaluation.

The biggest of these by far is the third, where we give you a detailed, guided tour of how to facilitate effectively. You don't just 'get in there and facilitate', mind you, (or if you do, don't blame us when it doesn't work!). Effective training doesn't happen in a vacuum and it's important to set the main ideas on facilitation in context. We do this by looking at the important 'befores and afters' about which you need to think and do something. These apply to **any** training event, not just one involving facilitation.

At the end of the book, we offer a small selection of further reading. This is given because all the ideas we present in this book are firmly rooted in adult learning theory.

> In making this book a **practical** guide we have deliberately left out abstract theoretical arguments and justifications.

There will, we guess, be many readers of this book who will want either to check the bona fides of our approach or to discover more about adult learning in general. The books we list in our Bibliography – a sample only – will be helpful to both types of reader.

Let's start, then, with a look at what sparks off a learning event for 'them', where 'them' is your staff, team, colleagues, subordinates – anyone for whom you are the responsible 'trainer'.

2 Training Needs Analysis

Imagine that you have set up the following lunchtime training 'events' for your team:

1 A session including an activity on communication skills, because you feel some of your team – though not all – need to improve their ability to get their ideas across, face to face. You *have not* discussed the reasons for this event with your team.

2 A session including an activity on communication skills, because some of the team – though not all – feel they need to improve their ability to get their ideas across, face to face. You *have* discussed the reasons for this event with your team.

Which is likely to be the more successful session, and why?

A moment's thought should suggest that the second event is much more likely to be successful, even though the content of both sessions might be identical.

You would probably want to argue, and you'd be right, that if certain team members have themselves seen a need to which you are responding, then they will see the benefit. Those team members who don't see they have a problem will almost certainly be happy to be involved in such a session on the basis that they will be contributing to team development by helping their colleagues meet their expressed needs.

Event 1 by comparison is fraught with potential problems. YOU may feel some team members have a need, but do THEY? Should you not have discussed it with them privately and agreed that some kind of training is the right way of tackling it? And what of the team members who feel they don't have a problem? Why, they will say, are we having to be trained in something we already know we're good at? All in all, this is the recipe for a fiasco.

There are two issues we want to get at here:

1 Training should *never* occur in a vacuum. It has to be seen as part of a wider scene – set in context. If its purpose is unclear to all but you as the trainer then it's rather like tossing people a loose piece of jigsaw without the other parts. It may be an interesting shape and with pretty colours, but where,

exactly, does it 'fit'? The Activities in this book can be seen as pieces of a jigsaw. Within this book they constitute a 'wider picture' but, taken out of context, what will they mean to your team?

2 Training Needs Analysis (TNA) is really such a fundamental process that we simply could not present a book like this without considering it. It is TNA that helps to set your training in the wider context. Without it, your training events will almost certainly lack purpose and benefit – they may be enjoyable to do, but will the time and effort really be worth it in the end? Without some kind of TNA, the answer will be a resounding 'No!'

TNA is often seen as the province of specialist trainers, but it's actually a process that all good managers indulge in all the time. In this part of the book we would like to offer a tried and tested approach to TNA, which we think will make sense intuitively but which should also give you considerably greater confidence when running a training event; a confidence which springs from knowing that your event has resulted from a proper TNA.

It's possible to see three main ways in which the need for a TNA might arise. It can result from:

1 **Some kind of corporate / organisational / business need**. The business might be changing, in whole or in part, or its procedures and practices may have been under review. Substantial, company-wide changes of culture, climate, image, practice and so on may be required. In such cases a TNA arises because employees need to acquire, enhance or change their

- knowledge
- skills
- attitudes

in order for the change to be effective and corporate objectives met.

2 **Some kind of job-related need**. The requirements of a job may change and evolve over time. For example, computerisation of much clerical and financial work in recent years has brought fundamental changes to jobs, in some cases removing the need for them altogether. Working practices alter as new machinery or systems become available. In order to carry out their job effectively, either because they are new to it or because the job has changed, the need for a TNA arises because employees need to acquire, enhance or change their

- knowledge
- skills
- attitudes

in order for the requirements of the job to be satisfied.

3 **The needs of individuals**. Although these may be related to 1 and/or 2 above, the need will emerge, not from business or job requirements directly, but rather from some kind of appraisal of the needs of an individual employee, probably done jointly by the employee and manager. These can either be seen as meeting *remedial* needs (there is some deficiency in observed or measured performance) or as meeting *developmental* needs, for example preparing the employee for career advancement. In either case the TNA will arise because the employee, or the manager, or both together, identify that the individual needs to acquire, enhance or change their

- knowledge
- skills
- attitudes

in order to fulfil the remedial or developmental need.

Common to all three of these viewpoints is the idea that training needs can be pigeon-holed into one of three types:

- training needed to acquire or develop **knowledge**
- training needed to acquire or develop **skills**
- training needed to acquire or develop **attitudes.**

This approach to TNA (sometimes known as KSA while we're into abbreviations) is a very familiar one.

However, before launching into a brief summary of accepted practice on TNA, you may like to think about the following questions BEFORE you embark on a TNA yourself. These questions are suggested by Rosemary Harrison in *Training and Development* (*see* Bibliography).

1 **Is training really the answer at all?** Do I have a problem relating to some other factor, such as poor supervision, incapacity, personal problems and so on? Training may not always be an appropriate response, in which case a TNA will be a waste of time.

2 **Is training actually the most cost-effective answer?** Would it be cheaper/better to buy in the expertise required, for example, to carry out a very specialised, one-off task, or is there some other non-training solution?

3 **Has this investigation already been carried out before?** Is there data and/or an analysis available to you without further investigation, for example has some analysis already been done by a colleague with a similar situation elsewhere in the business or by a predecessor or by a central training department?

4 **How much change is likely to occur over time?** Only spend time doing a full analysis where the results are not going to be invalid very quickly.

5 **Should the job be adapted to the person, rather than the other way round?** Maybe a reallocation of duties might be a much more effective way of resolving a problem than by trying to change someone's personality overnight!

We shall assume, then, that you have answered these questions and still believe a TNA is necessary.

What are the implications of a KSA analysis for you as trainer, and how do you actually carry out a Training Needs Analysis which identifies training needs in KSA terms? There are four types of approach, three of which are likely to be relevant to readers of this book.

1 **The comprehensive analysis**, as its name suggests, involves an in-depth analysis of all tasks required to be actioned within a business/unit/section/ team and so on. This can lead to the preparation of a detailed profile of the knowledge, skills and attitudes required for each individual job. For the most part this will only occur rarely, such as when a new team is to be set up, or a new factory opened, or brand new skills are required in order to operate a new system.

   The technique requires time and commitment, and will result in the writing/revision of job descriptions and personnel specifications (what the job holder should be able to do). This, in turn, leads to the preparation of training syllabuses and course delivery.

2 **Key task analysis** along with the next type, is the most likely to confront readers of this book. The approach involves looking at a specific job and identifying the key tasks required by it. A personnel specification can then be drawn up which will suggest the KSA requirements.

Example

Suppose one key task of a security guard is to challenge anyone not wearing an approved identity pass. What might be the personnel specification implications of such a key task?

Your own thoughts may differ from ours, but we might include:

- sensitivity but firmness
- good interpersonal skills
- reasonable physical presence and fitness.

While the last of these is perhaps more to do with selection criteria than with training, the first two might certainly imply training needs. If we take the KSA approach, these might emerge as follows:

Knowledge
- who's who in the company
- company rules and procedures for employees and visitors on premises
- company policy for dealing with intruders

Skills
- good oral communication skills
- assertion skills in dealing with potentially difficult encounters
- ability to defend oneself if attacked

Attitudes
- firmness but fairness
- preference to avoid hostile confrontation
- company interests seen as important.

All of these are amenable to training, of course, and the value of the KSA analysis lies in being able to break down the needs under headings. The next section will look (continuing to use this example) at how KSA can help to suggest appropriate ways of responding.

3 **Problem-centred analysis** is unrelated to needs resulting from corporate or job requirements but is rather a response to the identification of a deficiency in individuals or teams. In the case of our security guard, persistent complaints about rudeness or inappropriately aggressive challenging of visitors would result in a problem-centred analysis.

'Problems' may be identified by others or by individuals themselves. Either way, the training response will be to the problem (deficiency in performance) rather than some kind of task analysis.

4 **Core analysis** is more related to the provision of, say, core skills in order to meet an external training requirement or nationally recognised qualification, and is beyond the scope of this book.

What methods of TNA are open to you in order to determine KSA requirements for optimum performance? There are five main ones. Use any that seem appropriate to your situation. None are mutually exclusive and you can use several in combination.

1 **Observation** involves simple watching and assessing the performance of the employee carrying out an identified task.

2 **Self-observation** can be useful but depends on the willingness by the employee to keep accurate 'diaries' for later analysis.

3 **Questionnaires** are especially useful as a preliminary to the next method, but they do need to be drawn up by people who understand what they are doing.

4 **Fact-finding interview** is probably the most extensively used method. Invaluable and essential, provided the person conducting the interview has good questioning and listening skills. Interviews will almost certainly need to be conducted with a wide range of people – senior management, the post holder, internal customers and so on.

5 **Trying it for yourself** involves carrying out a task personally in order to experience what is involved.

This chapter has been a very brief overview of TNA. For a much more in-depth analysis, please refer to Kenney and Reid's *Training Interventions* and/or Rosemary Harrison's *Training and Development*.

Landmark

Question	Notes
Where does the apparent need for a TNA originate?	
Is a TNA actually the best response to the situation?	
Should I analyse the job or the individual?	
What method(s) should I use for the analysis?	
After the TNA, have I been able to identify the Knowledge, Skills and Attitudes requirements which I need to tackle?	

3 From training needs to learning objectives

Beginning with this section we shall call 'trainees' participants, in order to be consistent with the Activities in Part Two and to reflect more properly a major feature of facilitation, that of learner participation.

Having decided what knowledge, skills and attitudes need to be learned, practised and/or developed the next stage is to start to think about how to meet these identified needs. The best way – indeed, the only way if the training is to be guaranteed the best chance of success – is to draw up a list of learning objectives. This simply means asking the question: What should the participant be able to do after the training has been carried out?

Let's return to our example of the security guard from the previous section.

Example

In terms of knowledge we suggested that there might be at least three possible needs to know:

- who's who in the company
- company rules and procedures for employees and visitors on premises
- company policy on dealing with intruders.

Learning objectives – what the participant should be able to do – might in this case read as follows:

Knowledge objectives
By the end of the training event the participant should:

- know the names of company personnel designated as key and be able to recognise them from photographs
- know that the Company Internal Directory exists and understand how to access its information
- understand and be able to apply company procedures for admission of staff to the premises

---

- understand and be able to apply company procedures for dealing with visitors
- know and understand the basic legal rights afforded to the company in order to be able to deal effectively with intruders
- know and understand a range of actions relating to intruders which are not permitted under the law or company policy.

We can adopt a similar approach to the skills requirements:

Skills objectives
By the end of the training event the participant should be able to:

- communicate orally in an effective manner with the full range of company personnel and with visitors
- be able to handle difficult, demanding and unreasonable personnel and visitors in a tactful but effective manner, using appropriate assertion skills
- be able to apply self-defence skills in an emergency situation where personal danger would otherwise result.

Finally, the attitude requirements:

Attitude objectives
By the end of the training event the participant should:

- be able to adopt a firm, fair and non-aggressive approach in situations requiring sensitivity but where company security is at risk
- appreciate the potential dangers to the company and its personnel of unauthorised access.

These lists do not pretend to be comprehensive; they are merely included to give a flavour of how learning objectives might be drawn up.

It is from a list of learning objectives that a training event or course can be put together which attempts to meet the learning objectives. If you glance at some of the Activities in Part Two you will find each has a stated aim. The aim will, in each case, strongly suggest what the learning objectives of those undertaking the activity might be, though we have avoided spelling out precise objectives since we want the Activities to be used flexibly!

Having derived objectives, the next question, inevitably, is: How do I deliver training that will satisfy these objectives? A trainer planning a training event has to consider two issues – WHAT do the participants need to achieve (learning objectives) and HOW will I help them achieve it (what training techniques can I use)?

It's also reasonable to ask if some types of learning objective are better achieved through certain techniques than others. The short answer is that it is not easy to give a short answer! It is possible to break down the KSA approach further in order to see if this is helpful in provide guidance on matching objectives to technique.

Knowledge acquisition/development can be split into:

- comprehension – understanding of some kind of theoretical matter
- memorisation – remembering without necessarily understanding.

Skills acquisition/development can be split into:

- reflex-type skills – practical and manual dexterity
- procedural-type skills – following established guidelines or techniques.

Attitude acquisition/development/change probably belongs to a class on its own.

The table summarises some thoughts on matching objectives to techniques, using the fivefold split suggested above. We have chosen some of the most popular training techniques for this exercise. A YES entry indicates that a technique could make a valuable contribution to meeting a learning objective which reflects a need of the type shown. A NO entry indicates the reverse, while a '?' indicates that there will be occasions when it would be useful and others when it would not.

You may not agree with all of our analysis, but we believe there would be broad agreement on certain aspects. For example, few people these days believe that a lecture is an effective way to tackle attitude change, any more than interviewing skills (procedural) can be acquired by reading a textbook, or a grasp of computer program algorithms be obtained from a role play.

In thinking about the possible techniques to be used to meet learning objectives you will find yourself beginning to consider the design of the actual programme for the event or course. In terms of this book, we have provided Activities which are designed, mainly, for 'one-off' learning events, and so the question of structure does not really arise unless you are putting together something longer. (Each activity has already been organised for you to make for an effective learning experience in its own right).

Do consider, too, the need for balance and change of pace in designing your programme. Effective training and facilitation reflects thought on these items.

Technique	Compre-hension	Memor-isation	Reflex skills	Proced-ural skills	Attitudes
Listening to a lecture	YES	?	NO	NO	NO
Sitting 'next to Nellie'	?	YES	YES	NO	NO
Watching a demon-stration	YES	NO	?	?	NO
Reading a textbook	YES	?	NO	NO	NO
Group discussion	?	NO	NO	?	YES
Watching a video	YES	NO	NO	?	NO
Following a technical/ user manual	YES	?	?	YES	NO
Computer-based training	YES	YES	YES	YES	NO
Role plays	NO	NO	?	YES	YES
Case study	YES	NO	NO	?	YES
Practical activity/ game	?	NO	YES	YES	?

In other words, an event needs to include many elements – ice-breakers, trainer input, discussion, role play, exercises and so on. Avoid over-long discussions or programming several similar activities 'back to back'.

Landmark

Question	Notes
Have I translated my KSA analysis into clear learning objectives?	
What techniques should I consider using to meet each of the learning objectives?	
Do I plan to use a sufficient variety of techniques so that there is a balance and changes of pace throughout my proposed event?	

4 The skills of facilitation

INTRODUCTION

Having looked very briefly at the processes which lead up to an effective learning event, we now take a much more detailed look at the process of facilitation. All of the Activities in Part Two of this book require facilitation. So, exactly what is facilitation? Before defining it, we need to think of the setting in which facilitation takes place – the group.

GROUP ISSUES

A group of people is always unpredictable – the behaviour of individuals will be affected by the group and vice versa. People will, at times, behave differently in a group to the way they would normally behave with you or with other colleagues. It's this phenomenon which makes facilitation exciting, and always a challenge. One thing you will discover early on is that, however well you plan things – anticipate group and individual reactions – there will always be the element of surprise. It's easy to be thrown by this. The Activities should give you a sense of security, for they are all tried and tested and the guidance we offer you on each one is rooted in our own experience of facilitation, so we have identified some of the potential pitfalls. But we can NEVER identify all of them, nor can you. So be prepared for the unexpected! (In this chapter we shall offer you some thoughts on how to handle the unexpected without panic.)

There are four aspects to working with groups which we feel have a special bearing on your dual role as manager and facilitator.

Group synergy

It is this elusive concept that so often defeats football managers who strive to put together a winning team of individually excellent players. It shows itself in work teams made up of talented people, but the overall performance of the team may be below what was expected. Group synergy is what happens when a team is actually less than, or more than, the sum of its individual parts. It's a result of a 'rogue' element which it is difficult, if not impossible, to either see in advance or make allowances for. As a group facilitator you will come to know the mysteries of group synergy! Meredith Belbin has done some very interesting work on management teams (*Management Teams: Why They Succeed or Fail*). He succeeded in 'taking apart' teams which were unsuccessful, despite being composed of, perhaps, individually excellent people. He isolated the reasons for poor performance and was able to make predictions about how to put together successful teams. His analysis is as close to pinning down this elusive idea of synergy as any and you should read his book if this aspect of groups interests you.

What you must expect is that your work team, made up of individuals, and possibly even already working well together as a work team, may not necessarily perform as you anticipate in a team training event. Don't be caught out by this – we can almost guarantee it.

Stages in group cohesion

It takes any team time to settle down and establish itself, and this is just as true when you put a work team into a training situation, which will most likely be unfamiliar to them. You may find it helpful to know that there is a recognised series of stages through which a work (or training) team will normally pass *en route* to becoming effective. These are defined as:

● forming
● storming
● norming
● performing.

These stages are well documented and well accepted and, as both a manager of a new work team and certainly as a group facilitator, you ignore these stages at your peril! So what do they mean?

Forming

This is when the group comes together for the first time, either as an established group unfamiliar with each other, or as a new group in an unfamiliar situation (such as a team training event). There will be visible signs of anxiety and dependence on the leader. There is also likely to be a 'testing out' of the situation and a search for what constitutes acceptable behaviour.

Storming

Often the most difficult stage for the leader. Conflict can arise, especially between smaller groups or factions within the team. The leader's role may be resented and opinions become extreme and polarised. The group may actually resist attempts to control it.

Norming

The group begins to 'hang together' and conflicts are resolved. A sense of mutual support and group identity begins to emerge and, along with them, a willingness to join in an open exchange of views and feelings. The mood moves towards co-operative effort. Good facilitators value ice-breakers in training unfamiliar groups simply because they often help to short-circuit the worst effects of forming and storming, letting the group experience the 'good vibes' which normally only begin to occur at the norming stage.

Performing

Any relationship problems between individual team members get patched up here. Things get done through mutual effort and use of 'interpersonal' techniques. Team roles become more flexible and the overall climate is focused towards problem-solving. High energy levels abound.

Your work team and you, as facilitator, in a training situation

One of the inevitable truths when a manager takes on the role of training their team in a group situation, and attempts to be a facilitator, is that it will never work 100 per cent . Sorry about that, but it's unrealistic to expect anything else.

The advantage that *external* training facilitators bring to facilitating training activity for existing teams is the ability to be seen as 'honest brokers' – not to side with any one individual or faction and to offer unbiased comment on what is happening. (We consider the role of facilitator later in this chapter.) You, on the other hand, will naturally have been involved with all of your team on a day-to-day basis, and they will never be able to totally divorce your managerial role from the role you are trying to play as facilitator. Of course, this doesn't mean you can't facilitate effectively, but it does place certain limitations on what you can expect to achieve. And if you try to 'join in' *as an equal*, perhaps in an exercise, this will never work, unless you have a very unusual team.

Be open to learning yourself

A definite bonus, this! When you facilitate a group, and perhaps especially one made up of people you work with on a daily basis, you will find that YOU end up learning as well. You will have set learning objectives for your group, but you should always reflect, after a training session where you have been a facilitator, on what YOU have learned, either in terms of your facilitator skills or about your team or about people within it. You may surprise yourself.

The purpose of all this material on groups is not to frighten you off – people are nervous enough about trying out facilitation for the first time without us making it worse. It is rather to alert you to some realities which it is difficult to avoid. That way, at least, you can understand what is going on as it happens, notably when things are not happening as you feel they should.

So let us turn now to look in detail at this exciting, unpredictable, developmental process which we have mentioned repeatedly, but not yet defined: facilitation. We have divided up what follows into two sections; the first defines what (good) facilitation is all about. The second consists of a series of short sections which emphasise some of the many practical issues which have to be dealt with if facilitation is to be effective.

SO, EXACTLY WHAT IS FACILITATION?

The problem with answering this apparently simple question is that there is a lot of debate and argument among academics and practitioners about what facilitation really means. Whole books have been written about it (we recommend Stephen Brookfield's) and it would be trite for us to suggest that there is a simple answer. Theories of adult education have a strong bearing on it, but it is not our intention to go into those in this, essentially practical, book.

A dictionary definition of facilitation would run along the lines of 'To promote or make easy'. This is helpful, because the kind of facilitation with which the authors of this book are familiar, and which we want to promote through the Activities, is about enabling something to happen easily. (The 'something' is, of course, the achievement of those learning objectives.)

There is more to it than that, of course. A lecture could be seen as making learning easy in appropriate circumstances yet we don't count lecturing as facilitation. We get closer to it with the idea that the more traditional training methods, of the 'chalk and talk' variety, are basically unsuited to achieving change within individual participants, except in the limited sense of perhaps adding to their knowledge of a topic. Training frequently demands much more than that: changes in attitude, acquisition of new skills, new ways of looking at things. These changes are normally easier to achieve through participative learning.

What do we mean by participative learning? In essence, we are talking about learning in which individual participants take some responsibility for their own learning. The trainer is not seen as having all the responsibility. Participative learning implies a decision to take part in active learning, where there is a commitment to join in, to learn and to display a sense of involvement. The notion of being spoonfed by the trainer is anathema to a participative learning experience. Participative training methods (on which all of the Part Two activities are based) are more likely to achieve these aims, and participative training methods require facilitation.

But we need to stop here and justify (briefly) just *why* participative learning methods are more likely to work in these circumstances. A widely accepted view (held by many in the adult learning field) is that, in order to create a good learning climate for adults, the facilitator must:

- allow adult learners the freedom and opportunity to contribute to, and influence, the learning process
- allow adults to draw on their own experience (of life, work and so on) and to have it valued
- ensure the learning objectives are clearly relevant to real-life tasks and problems
- allow adults to see the relevance and practical application of the learning to their own real-life situations

There is much academic debate about whether these four assumptions make up the bones of a respectable learning theory for adults, and if you want to explore the ideas further, refer to Brookfield's, *Understanding and Facilitating Adult Learning*.

For our purposes, the above four assumptions form a useful basis for 'doing' facilitation well. If you allow them to influence how you design and deliver your participative learning event, then it will stand the best chance of succeeding. What, then, might be some of the practical implications of these four assumptions for you as facilitator? We suggest the following main ones, though you may be able to think of more yourself.

Implications for facilitation in practice

- Adults need to be involved in analysing the learning need, in setting learning objectives and in sharing responsibility for learning and evaluation.
- Adults need a supportive learning climate.
- Adults learn from each other, not just from the 'teacher'; adults are a rich resource for learning. For example, it is not uncommon for as much learning to take place in a chat over coffee, as participants reflect on what they have done, as in the more formal learning setting.
- Evaluation of learning should be in terms of 're-diagnosis of need' rather than 'pass or fail'.

- New learning will be related to experience; adults may appear less open-minded than younger learners.
- Experiential learning techniques may work better in some situations than more formal, transmittal (or lecturing) techniques.
- Emphasising the application of learning in the 'real world' will be a major factor in the success of adult learning.
- Learning is likely to be more powerful if it uses as its focus some kind of problem or issue which needs solving or addressing. More general, abstract approaches may work less well.
- The starting point for all adult learning should be the issues and concerns which adults bring with them.

We're now in a position to define facilitation in terms of good practice. Drawing together the threads of what we have been outlining above, we offer the following guide.

Effective facilitation requires:

- an acknowledgement by the facilitator that the decision to learn is voluntary, and that bullying, humiliation, coercion and so on do not work.
- respect among participants (including the facilitator) for each other's self-worth. This is absolutely critical. Good facilitation aims to enhance self-worth. Abuse, laughing at individuals or groups (as opposed to with them), putting people down, exposing people's vulnerability and weaknesses to ridicule – all are 'off limits' to a good facilitator.
- a sense of co-operation to exist between all participants and the facilitator. This must allow for flexibility especially in content terms. New avenues may need to be explored, agendas renegotiated where a new need emerges.
- a cycle of doing/reflecting/analysing/doing . . . to be at the heart of adult learning. It's certainly at the heart of many of the activities in Part Two. It means allowing participants to try doing something, then reflecting on how it went, then analysing the 'doing' phase, looking for any possible improvements and/or different possible approaches, then trying it again. The cycle can be repeated as often as necessary.
- critical questioning of existing situations and ways of doing things in order to encourage new ways of seeing things that were previously just accepted.
- facilitation to be about empowering individuals to take control over their relationships and their work worlds rather than being reactive and accepting.

If we were to be asked to tease out the most important of this, potentially very powerful, set of principles' then we would probably want to emphasise the following critical requirement:

A good group facilitator recognises and values the experience which individual group participants bring, and understands the importance of group and individual contributions to the learning event and any action which is to follow it.

If you find yourself in the position of not being able to value your participants and recognise that they, too, have something to offer, then you will not make a good facilitator. If you belong to the school which says that the trainer must know everything there is to know about a subject and the participants know nothing, then you will not make a good facilitator. If you enjoy dominating people, then you will not make a good facilitator. If you are actually frightened of the idea that a group may want to 'change the learning agenda' and explore something relevant but not anticipated by you in advance, then you will not make a good facilitator.

We could go on and on, for it's easy to list those failings that make for a poor facilitator. Can we, though, identify what makes a *good* facilitator (as opposed to facilitation good practice)?

The following list will serve.

An effective group facilitator will:

- be concerned about, and for, the learners
- value the experience which learners bring with them and help them, in turn, to value it also
- be knowledgeable in their subject
- be able to relate theory to practice
- appear confident
- be open to exploring and trying out different approaches
- present an honest and open personality to the group
- go beyond set objectives when required
- create a good atmosphere for learning
- be aware of the distinction between content and process (see below) and be able to contribute positively to both.

This is, if you like, a 'creed', or statement of belief. Think of effective group trainers you may have worked with. Can you identify any, or perhaps all, of these characteristics in such people? Or think of group trainers who you feel have been ineffective. Did they fail on several of these criteria? The answer is, probably, yes. It's this 'creed' that lies behind all of the Activities we have devised for this book, in particular the 'processing' notes we supply with them.

Since we have mentioned 'content' and 'process' in the above list but without actually describing what we mean, it's important now to consider this. While the group itself is most likely (if not exclusively) to be concerned with 'content', the facilitator has to be constantly aware of both. The distinction between content and process is a fundamental one and its importance cannot be overemphasised, since it is a distinction that will help you to understand better what's happening in your group and to know how to tackle group effectiveness problems.

From the moment you start to formulate learning objectives you are working on content. When you move into delivery you are still working with content but you will be beginning to concentrate on process. During the training event itself, you, as facilitator, are likely to be concentrating on both process and content while the participants will be concentrating on content.

So what does all this mean?

Training content is, in essence, the subject being considered by the group. So, if you are running an event designed to allow participants to practice self-defence techniques, the techniques themselves, and their application and practice, would be the training content.

Training process is, in essence, the 'stage management' of the training process. In the self-defence example, the style of the trainer and its impact on the group (whether humour is used or not, whether shy individuals feel inhibited, and so on) would be an example of process. The relationships between individual participants and the extent to which this helps or hinders learning is process. A final example would be the choice of training techniques (note, NOT the self-defence techniques themselves) – such as the manner in which demonstrations are carried out, or safe practice is encouraged and monitored, or individual coaching is offered.

Facilitation of an activity or exercise requires five clear stages. These are all contained within the processing notes for the Activities in Part Two but we think it sensible to list them here:

- *Introduce the activity, saying something about why you are using it.*
- *Run it.*
- *Afterwards, 'unpack' it, getting some first reactions.*
- *Draw out the learning points and make them explicit.*
- *Consider how to apply the learning points to 'real' life back at work.*

We really can't stress enough the importance of NOT just taking an activity 'off the shelf', running it and then leaving participants to draw their own conclusions.

An often used technique for facilitators is to stop an exercise or discussion and pose a question along the lines of: 'Can we stop and think about what's happening here?'. This is an invitation to the group to stop thinking of content and to reflect on process.

We shall finish this section with a brief outline of one further way of analysing the important facilitation skill of 'process' awareness and analysis. It's possible to spot two different (but related) process functions at work in a group. These are:

- task functions
- maintenance functions.

Task functions are actions, carried out by the group, that contribute directly to the progress of the task being worked on (content). Examples of task functions are:

- information giving and seeking – sharing of information relevant to the task and asking questions to elicit information
- making proposals – offering suggestions and ideas on subjects such as the planning and organisation of tasks, allocating work, setting objectives and prioritising tasks
- summarising discussions – keeping group members informed and up to date, and checking mutual understanding of progress and current position
- evaluating – assessing the suitability of ideas and proposals before final decisions are taken
- giving direction – can fall to others rather than the actual group leader, or the facilitator.

So, task functions, taking these examples, make a clear contribution to the achievement of the task in hand – they are the 'tools to do the job'. *Maintenance functions*, however, are more closely identified with group cohesion – ways of binding the group together, of ensuring that the task functions are carried out well. Examples of maintenance functions would be:

- encouraging participation – bringing others in, checking out agreement, seeking out opinions and views (especially important in order to encourage more diffident or reluctant group members to feel they have a valued contribution to make)
- communicating and listening – listening actively, i.e. not interrupting others, clarifying their thinking where necessary and ensuring that all members of the group are involved (for example, regular eye contact with all group members)
- relieving tension – reducing tension at times of inevitable conflict and differences of opinion, especially, perhaps, at times when difficult decisions have to be made

- trust building – valuing the judgement of others and accepting it, delegating tasks (and letting people get on with it), maintaining confidentiality when requested, avoidance of such behaviours as scapegoating and putting individuals down

- process awareness and reflection – understanding what is going on, giving and accepting feedback on how people are feeling and performing and being able to reflect on possible alternative behaviours.

We hope these brief thoughts will offer a glimpse of what we want to advocate by way of effective facilitation. What follows represents a step-by-step guide to becoming a good facilitator. Good luck – it really is one of the most rewarding things you can do if you can get it right. But although there may be a sense of personal reward, the true reward should come from the satisfaction that your participants have achieved their learning objectives. Be warned! It's distinctly possible that they may not truly realise just how important a role you played in that process. Such is the nature of true facilitation in action.

But just before we move on, a Landmark on this part of the chapter which poses some fundamental questions for you.

Landmark

Question	Notes
What do I understand by the four stages of group cohesion (Forming/Storming/Norming/Performing)?	
Am I prepared, as facilitator, to admit that I might have something to learn from my involvement in a learning event?	
What does good facilitation practice require in a group situation?	
Do I know, believe in and passionately want to put into practice the effective group facilitator's 'creed'?	
What do I understand the difference to be between content and process?	
What do I understand the difference between group task and group maintenance functions to be?	

We now move into the second section of this chapter, which is very different from the more general material on facilitation so far. In what follows we set out practical, down-to-earth guidelines. They are based on two main sources:

- good training and facilitation practice
- the authors' own experiences.

You will probably recognise the latter for we have tried to make several serious points in a somewhat tongue-in-cheek way. We've done this partly to counterbalance the somewhat heavier material which has preceded this part of the book but also to make a number of points in a fairly graphical (and, hopefully, memorable) way.

Taken together with the Activities, and the suggestions on how to process them (contained within each Activity), we aim to create here a basic 'user guide' to facilitating the Activities we provide. Our longer-term aim is to provide a sound basis so that you may try out, practise and develop your facilitation skills, grow in self-confidence, and progress to being a good facilitator. In doing this you will come to your own conclusions about techniques that work for you and which you can use to foster a good learning climate.

The headings which follow are:

- **Befores** – a list of things to do before you facilitate your event
- **The learning environment** – physical issues to do with rooms, seating and so on
- **Resources** – the equipment and any other material you may need
- **Starting a learning event** – your group is assembled; try not to panic!
- **How to use the Activities in this book** – a few thoughts on making the best use of the material in Part 2
- **Examples of good facilitation in practice** – some specific examples of what all the material introduced earlier in this section means in reality
- **Outcomes and action plans** – ideas on how to avoid spoiling a good event as a result of failure to follow through.

We're presenting each section in a new layout and then, at the very end of Part 2, each section will be summarised by means of a Checklist (as opposed to a Landmark).

We do not claim that the material which follows is comprehensive. It never can be for so much will depend on your group, your situation, your needs, their needs, the facilities available to you and so on. However, we have tried to include the principal items which, if you fail to attend to them, can undermine even your best efforts at facilitation.

BEFORES

▶ **Is training the answer to your problem?**

You should consider if the apparent learning need, wherever it stems from, can be more suitably met by some means other than training. Only move to the next stage if you are satisfied that training is the right solution.

▶ **Training Needs Analysis.**

We hope that, by now, it goes without saying that, before considering any kind of learning event, you need to have carried out a Training Needs Analysis!

▶ **Learning objectives.**

Have you translated your TNA into learning objectives? To what extent have you involved your potential learners in this process? Have you told them you are considering a training response to a problem? Do they recognise the problem and have a sense of 'ownership' over it (i.e. do they see it as a problem, too)? If not, you may need to convince them first. Once convinced you would be well-advised to involve them directly in deriving the learning needs. You'll find the process so much simpler if you do and, provided it's a proper consultation exercise, you will gain early commitment to the learning event.

▶ **Design your learning event.**

This may be best done alone, especially if you are going to use case studies or other material which is best not accessed in advance. Think of how you are going to provide a programme which will have a sense of balance (not too many similar things together) and pace (allowing appropriate time). Allow especially for teams with 'doers' rather than 'thinkers'. Some participants will find it really hard to sit around discussing things, especially if they are 'doers' – used to practical things.

Consider, too, as you design your event, the practical aspects – such as who else needs to know or be consulted about your plans to run an event lasting, perhaps, through a lunch time or beyond? Other managers? More senior personnel? Internal customers who may be affected?

▶ **Are there any participants with special circumstances?**

At the design stage it's important to assess if any of your participants have special circumstances which require particular support during the learning event. Apart from obvious things like sight or hearing defects or other physical disabilities, what about people who may have a problem reading? Several of our activities require an ability to read, sometimes quite large amounts of material. Are you going to allow enough time for slow readers or do you need to consider some form of help? You might consider reading it out loud yourself, provided the whole group is not alienated and does not see it as patronising.

Assuming you can be open with the people concerned, ask them if there is any way in which you can offer additional support. Don't overlook problems or make assumptions about solutions – check with those affected!

▶ Brief your participants.

If you have involved them in the design of the event, your briefing task will be easier, but, if you have not, you need to ensure that they all understand the purpose of the learning event and its objectives. You will need to ensure, in advance of the event, that they can perceive the relevance and understand how it fits into any wider team or individual development plans you may have. See this stage as a two way process – try not to only 'tell them'. You may need to engage in a dialogue and clarify objectives (for example) at the briefing stage.

Don't forget that you may need to involve other managers in the briefing process if your event is not solely for your own staff. Try also to offer some thoughts on what is likely to happen after the event is over.

▶ Joining instructions.

Organise some form of written confirmation – memo, e-mail, handwritten note – something. Confirm the date, time, duration and location. Ensure your participants know if they need to bring anything with them by way of material, pens, paper and so on, or if they need to do any reading, thinking or research before attending.

Be sure you deal firmly and clearly with issues involving time away from the desk – applications for leave on the day of the event, proposals to set up other meetings, visits and so on. In fairness to people with busy diaries you do need to give reasonable notice of your learning event, but do make it quite clear that it is assigned 'top priority' so that potential defaulters know where they stand.

In setting a date and time, you will clearly want to take into account:

● known leave commitments

● known meetings and other unavoidable situations which would prevent people attending

● cover for the workplace if all the team is involved and the event is during working hours

● if the event is to be during a lunch time or at the end of a day, that no one will be adversely affected by this. Try to resolve any potential difficulties (for example, someone needing to leave promptly each day to meet a child from school).

Avoid issuing too detailed a programme – this simply gives the more pedantic participants an excuse to challenge you on your timekeeping.

THE LEARNING ENVIRONMENT

▶ **Select the venue for the event with considerable thought.**

It really won't do to try to facilitate a learning event in some corner of the office or workshop where normal working life carries on regardless. On the other hand, we're not suggesting a need for fancy conference suites or hotels. What you need to do is to choose a room which satisfies the following criteria:

- quiet
- soundproof (beware temporary partitions or open-plan offices – you will get disturbed or you will disturb others)
- will not be affected by tradesmen working close by (hammering, metal sheets being sawn through, pneumatic drills in the basement . . .)
- adequately heated (not too hot or too cold)
- well lit, if possible with daylight. Beware rooms with fierce sun glare (will become a greenhouse) or very interesting views (participants' attention may wander)
- decently furnished. You cannot hope to convince your participants that you value them if you run your event in squalid surroundings
- the furniture 'matches', e.g. you do not have a mixture of different chair types or chairs which make it impossible to sit comfortably at tables (if the latter is required)
- clean and tidy, i.e. not a space cleared in a storage area full of crates and boxes and with cobwebs dangling from the light fittings
- adequate facilities for any special resources, e.g. power points for overhead projectors, blackout blinds for slide/video shows and so on
- there are no 'buzzing' fluorescent light fittings.

▶ **Think about how you want the room to be laid out and tell anyone who needs to know.**

Unless you specify you run the risk (if it's someone else's accommodation) of huge expanses of pine conference tables, a lectern, dais and microphone system for your intimate group session for yourself and five colleagues. Another favourite alternative is the setting-out of chairs and tables 'classroom style', in rows, all facing the front.

For almost all of the Activities in Part Two you should aim to:

- have comfortable easy chairs for yourself and your participants (do any of them have back problems which need upright chairs?)
- ensure you sit in a chair of the same height as everyone else – don't indulge in power games by looking down on them. And don't take the only comfortable chair, either!

- arrange the chairs in a horseshoe shape (if you are going to use a flipchart, for example) or in a circle (for discussion) so that everyone can see everyone else. Eye contact is important in group work

- have a table for any material such as handouts but avoid setting this up so that you sit behind it, like 'teacher'. This sets up a real barrier between you and your participants which will militate against good facilitation

- if tables are needed for people to work on during the event (but not all the time), try and arrange for them to be placed around the edges of the room rather than in the middle

- ensure that no one will be peering directly into the sunlight.

▶ **Make arrangements for refreshments.**
The arrival of noisy tea trolleys, rattling china and tea personnel can be a major distraction. (On the other hand, the non-arrival or non-existence of such items – crucial to the well-being of your group! – can be just as distracting.) It may be best to organise your own to be taken as and when you want them.

▶ **Ensure you – and *especially* your participants – will be interruption free.**
Interruptions are one of the worst nightmares of a good facilitator. Learning events in or near the normal workplace are usually plagued with them. 'Oh, Harry's only on a course up on the first floor. Pop up and see him, I'm sure he won't mind . . .' and so on. Interruptions and / or people being called out destroy the flow and they affect group cohesion. If someone is called away in mid-session then it is often (and rightly) perceived as an insult to the group (which feels itself to be less important than the interruption). More than two interruptions in one session and you will likely have a riot on your hands, and deservedly so.

1 Make it plain to your participants beforehand that you will brook no interruptions unless as a matter of life or death.

2 Try to stop anyone 'just popping back to the desk to see if there are any messages' while you take a short coffee break. You may never see them again until the event is over.

3 Take steps to prevent the outside world intruding, for example:

- You could try to ensure that the room is beyond the range of the internal paging system.

- Give your participants permission (if you can) to switch off their paging devices.

- Brief secretaries, receptionists and anyone else prone to cause interruption that you do not want to be disturbed.

- Disconnect any telephones in the room, if possible.

- Try putting a 'DO NOT DISTURB' notice on the door.
- Check the position on fire drills or alarm testing, especially in an unfamiliar venue.

and so on.

▶ **Check availability of separate syndicate rooms if needed.**
If there are none, ensure the main room is large enough to sustain more than one group working independently without disturbance from other groups.

▶ **If you have ordered resources (e.g. projectors, sound equipment etc.) from someone else, make sure they are compatible with the room and that the people responsible for supplying them know your needs well in advance.**
If you are counting on the provision of a flipchart and one is not evident when you arrive, you may find that such items are rarely available without a good deal of grovelling, begging and general aggravation.

▶ **The day before your event, check *everything* to do with the room.**
i.e. while you still have time to retrieve the situation. You do not want to turn up with your team and then have to engage in a debate about whether your team or the Board of Directors has prior claim on the room. 'But everyone knows the Board meets on the third Thursday of the month'. And, of course, you did but no one thought to remind you and it wasn't in the booking diary at the time.

RESOURCES

▶ **When planning your event give serious consideration to the equipment requirements.**
Identify them early and check their availability. Ensure they are 'compatible' with the training room. For example, is there a power point handy for the overhead projector. Will you need an extension lead? What about the screen, or can you get away with projecting on to a pale-coloured wall?

▶ **Ensure you give adequate notice of your requirements for handouts, copies of exercises and so on, or prepare them yourself as appropriate.**
In the Activities these are always made explicit at the beginning. You will find it essential to prepare such a list for any requirements beyond just 'paper and pens'.

▶ **Ensure there will be adequate supplies of paper, pens and any other stationery for your participants (and you) to use.**
If you are using an informal layout you might like to think of supplying clipboards for any written exercises or for note-taking.

▶ **Consider the idea of creating an emergency kit.**
For example, containing:

- scissors
- Blu-Tak
- sellotape
- spare pens and pencils
- erasers
- marker pens
- overhead projector pens

and so on. You'll be surprised how often you need these things!

▶ **Check out any equipment supplied well before your event starts.**
The following are common problems which face facilitators and which can cause an unnecessary rush of blood to the head:

- The flipchart stand you ordered is supplied. Flipchart paper is, however, absent and is locked away. The secretary who has the key is away sick today (of course).
- The flipchart stand has a pad of paper as required. All but the last three sheets are already covered in creative scribblings from another course. No one knows where spare pads are kept.
- The flipchart and paper are fine but there are no marker pens.
- The flipchart, paper and pens appear fine. Unhappily all the pens dried out, apparently several months ago.
- If using a whiteboard, there will only be spirit-based markers available (which won't rub off).
- The overhead projector works splendidly until you switch it on for the third time. The bulb blows. There is no spare in evidence nor, it appears, is there one within five miles of the building.
- There will be copious supplies of overhead projector acetates (or not, as the case may be) but no suitable pens. Have you ever tried writing on a piece of acetate with a ballpoint pen?
- You have been supplied with a sophisticated camcorder to record some role

plays. You have been assured it is 'foolproof'. It's not, of course, as you will find to your cost.

● Coyly placed 'PAUSE' buttons have been the undoing of many a facilitator who has just failed to record a 30-minute role play.

● Role plays which you plan to record on video will each last at least 30 minutes and there will be three of them. The camcorder will only have a 60-minute tape inside it.

● Hired videos have a nasty habit of not turning up, or of turning up somewhere else, or of turning out to be 'Terminator 2' instead of your helpful video on handling conflict.

● The hired video will bore your participants rigid as you play through the first 12 minutes of 'plugs' for the video company's other products before you get to the bit you want.

● Each of your four sets of handouts turns out to have two less than you require.

● One handout has been collated in reverse order with the middle page upside down and page 5 missing altogether.

We could go on.

STARTING A LEARNING EVENT

▶ **Plan your opening moves with great care.**
You should pay particular attention to the following:

● Don't waste time at the beginning of an event – you or the participants may be inclined to indulge in an informal team meeting (well, it's so rare we all get together like this . . .).

● Settle people down and ensure all are comfortable.

● Know what you are going to say by way of introduction, and don't ramble on. The average attention span is about ten minutes.

● Cover any domestic issues which might need dealing with if in an unfamiliar venue (e.g. toilets, fire escape routes and so on).

● Allow for urgent or genuine questions, but don't go along with questions which are time-wasting or designed to postpone getting down to the main business.

▶ **Negotiate some ground rules for the event.**
These are important for establishing the right climate in which learning can take place. Consider particularly the following:

- smoking – rules?
- confidentiality – you, them – what are you willing to be bound by? Negotiate and agree it.
- timekeeping, especially for a longer event. Are people willing to make a commitment to be on time? This applies equally to you, especially over things like finishing times.
- behaviour rules – these might be appropriate, for example getting some kind of agreement that people will offer advice and constructive criticism and not indulge in fault-finding and 'put-downs'. Or perhaps showing respect for others' views without necessarily agreeing with them.
- participation – again, maybe you can secure a commitment to it?
- gain agreement not to waste the group's time by 'popping out' to deal with work issues (see above).

You might like to consider the idea of flipcharting a 'contract' which everyone is happy to subscribe to and which includes the above issues. Stick it up on the wall for all to see throughout the event.

▶ **Give serious consideration to flipcharting (in advance) the learning objectives and displaying them throughout the event.**
Useful as a reminder and as a way of ensuring everyone is clear as to the purpose of the event.

▶ **Think about whether some form of participant introductions are needed.**
Clearly most usually required where participants do not know each other.

▶ **Consider (in advance) whether some kind of ice-breaker could be needed and select it for use at this stage of the event.**
Ice-breakers are recognised training tools. With groups where individuals have never met, they usually prove invaluable in 'breaking the ice' (hence the term). With established groups you can consider ice-breakers which seek to establish a good climate among colleagues who know each other. It might be necessary for people to 'wind down' from their immediate work concerns and pressures and to adjust to the different pace and requirements of your learning event. A well-chosen ice-breaker will help focus everyone's thinking on the issue in hand and also get everyone to say something – important in encouraging naturally diffident participants.

HOW TO USE THE ACTIVITIES IN THIS BOOK

▶ **Read the selected Activity through at the event design stage and decide if it helps meet your learning objectives.**
Each Activity is described at the outset, along with an aim which should give you a good idea as to its suitability for your purposes.

▶ **Be familiar with the Activity well in advance and have it beside you as you facilitate it.**
The Activities have been designed to:

● offer a clear step-by-step structure

● offer advice on timing

● make suggestions on processing, for example by providing questions which could be used to stimulate discussion

● help you avoid some potential pitfalls.

▶ **Be flexible in the timings.**
We offer only guidance on timings, just to give you an idea. Don't hesitate to adjust the timings to suit the needs of your group as you go along.

▶ **Have copies of any Exercise and / or Handouts ready well in advance.**
Details are set out clearly in those Activities which require them. Generally speaking: **Exercises** involve material which the participants will work on during the Activity; **Handouts** summarise key points which the Activity tries to make and are for distribution (normally) after the Activity. Try to avoid issuing Handouts to people at the beginning – especially avoid placing them on people's chairs for when they arrive. This will cause confusion and lack of attention at the beginning.

▶ **Be familiar beforehand with the contents of the 'Trainer input' sections.**
These are designed to give you the necessary background to a short presentation (of facts, ideas, research etc.) to your group. They have not been 'scripted' and you should not treat them as such. You can kill off your credibility as a facilitator at a stroke if you appear to read verbatim from a script. Rather, use them as a basis for making your own notes in advance.

▶ **Use the flipchart in a professional manner**
This is the most common item of equipment to appear in the Activities. When using it do try to ensure:

- your writing is legible from a few feet away
- you don't stand in front of it while you're charting – stand to one side so all can see
- you remove and display charts which you feel would be useful to refer to again later
- that, after your event is over, you make sure you remove discarded sheets – you never know who will look at them next.

▶ **Make use of the 'Questions you might use' sections if they are helpful to you.**
One of the major anxieties facing any novice group facilitator is 'What if they don't say anything?' The questions we provide are designed to provoke a response. Use them as a 'crib' if you're stuck but it would be much better, on the whole, if you devise your own. That way you can make them directly relevant to your learning event and to the real-life situations facing your participants.

▶ **Read through the 'Trainer notes' section beforehand.**
In the Activities where these are included, they either take the form of background notes, exclusively for your use as facilitator, or, in some cases, you might like to use them as the basis for a handout.

EXAMPLES OF GOOD FACILITATION IN PRACTICE

▶ **Check that anyone with special circumstances has had their needs met before you start.**
For example, does any one in your group have a hearing difficulty, or poor vision? Have their needs been catered for?

▶ **Consider people's needs for refreshment or comfort breaks.**
If your session is to last more than 90 minutes, some kind of break will be needed.

▶ **Value individuals and their contributions. Make it plain you welcome questions and comments – and mean it!**
You can employ at least two specific techniques here:

1 Bring in people who may have been silent or quiet for a time. Don't corner them with an aggressive challenge ('And what do YOU think, Sid?') but just check out that they are happy with what is going on.
2 Refer back to specific contributions later when relevant. For example: 'This goes back to what Mary was saying earlier about . . .'.

Sometimes you may need to bring others in the group into line, especially if some are conditioned to 'never listening to what Pauline has to say'.

▶ **While encouraging contributions, don't allow rampant anecdotalism.**
You need to distinguish between valid examples and tedious anecdotes, which may fascinate the teller and bore everyone else rigid.

▶ **Avoid bad facilitation behaviours.**
Examples are: poking fun, abusing, putting down, belittling, accusing, patronising. Avoid anything which smacks remotely of racist or sexist language. Jokes, humour and sarcasm at a participant's expense seldom contribute to good learning.

You should also be aware that certain training techniques can trigger high anxiety levels. Don't stoke up this anxiety! For example, if you plan to use closed-circuit TV to record role plays, try to ensure you are sensitive to the considerable anxieties many people have about this technique.

It's also a good idea to avoid the term 'role play' when discussing one. Try telling the group you are going to ask them to 'act something out'. That way you will lessen the chances of the negative reactions which the very words 'role play' can trigger in some people. It's also all too easy to be tempted to intervene if things are not going as you planned or anticipated. If (nevertheless) good learning is occurring, hold back.

▶ **Watch people's eyes.**
The best clues as to whether people are involved, hostile, feeling out of it etc., are their eyes. Use your own eyes to establish and maintain regular eye contact with ALL of your group throughout the event. It helps you to keep them involved (and on their toes) and they will feel you value them if you look at them occasionally. Avoid, though, constantly looking at the one participant who seems the most amiable!

▶ **Watch for signs of stress in members of your group.**
Be alert to non-verbal behaviour generally. We have already mentioned eye contact. Watch also for uncomfortable shifting of position, heavy sighs, suppressed anger. Keep alert particularly for participants whom you sense are deliberately holding back or appear uninvolved or bored or antagonistic – they may be plotting subversive tactics for later on, or they may just feel uninvolved, unvalued or bored. You might need to consider tackling this. For example, you could say to the group: 'I sense Howard is not happy with this. Is there something you want to say, Howard?' or you could suggest to the group that they might like to acknowledge and deal with the problem.

▶ **Don't be afraid of silences.**

If you get no immediate response to a question, don't panic. Silences of even two or three seconds can seem like a lifetime to the facilitator, but people often need time to think and reflect, especially if there is some problem-solving going on. Don't jump in to fill the gap – it's easy to feel the need to maybe restate or rephrase a question, or to pose supplementaries. This can cause confusion.

▶ **If someone asks you a question to which you can't think of an immediate response, throw it back to the group.**

A good ploy, this, provided it's not a question that only you can legitimately answer. (In that event, if you really don't know the answer, say so, and undertake to find out. You can probably get away with this just once.) Even if you CAN supply the answer, try throwing the occasional one back to the group. It helps them to become involved, to feel valued. Often the group answers turn out to be much better than your own would have been! Be magnanimous in defeat – after all, this event is, for them, about their learning, not an ego trip for you. Try to avoid engaging in lengthy one-to-one dialogues with individual participants and which allow you to air your knowledge. This is not true facilitation.

▶ **Be alert to the need for flexibility throughout. You may need to explore unexpected avenues.**

This can happen for two main reasons.

The first, and most exciting, is when there is a genuine sense of creativity and excitement in your group, and novel ways of approaching problems and situations emerge which require a flexible response from you as well as the group.

The second can be quite disconcerting when it happens, but can be handled well enough if you recognise what is going on. A learning event which has been founded on a dodgy TNA will display signs of stress and you may well need to ask yourself whether the TNA (your own or someone else's) was inaccurate. Ask yourself if the programme is really meeting the needs of the group. There are three options open to you:

● carry on regardless

● abandon the event and reconvene at another date

● adapt on the spot without losing sight of the original learning objectives.

▶ **Ask yourself repeatedly what is going on in process terms in your group.**

This will mean you have to step back from what is happening and adopt an observer role. If you believe certain behaviours (task or maintenance functions) are causing problems or getting in the way it is your role to call attention to them. But use your judgement here. It may be more appropriate NOT to deal with it at the time, but to log it (preferably making a written note of it to remind you later) so that you can draw the group's attention to it at a suitable time when you are reflecting on the event.

You may find the following suggestions helpful here:

● Is everyone involved? Don't necessarily judge involvement by the yardstick of who is talking. Active listening is also a form of participation.

● Has anyone opted out?

● Are people sharing information co-operatively?

● Is there leadership within the group and is it being appropriately used without damaging others?

● Who is influencing others here? How? (A good facilitator will not be worried if they are not alone in being influential in the group.)

● Does this group have a good decision-making mechanism?

● Are people's feelings being acknowledged?

● How is conflict (if any) being dealt with, or is it being suppressed? If the latter what should I do about it?

● If the group is having problems, is it necessarily down to me, as facilitator, to address them, or does the group have a responsibility too?

▶ **Have a range of questioning techniques on which you can draw.**
You may like to glance through the Activity 'Questioning skills' and then consider the range of possible question types that are open to you to use in your facilitation role.

▶ **If you need to give negative feedback, ensure you offer some constructive criticism at the same time.**
You may need to practise giving critical feedback in a way that leaves the individual or group feeling supported and with a positive learning result. For example: 'I thought the way John tackled that problem was great in principle, but the outcome was probably not what he wanted. How could he have done things differently?' A useful approach, this, when John has made a complete foul-up of something.

OUTCOMES AND ACTION PLANS

▶ **Because application of learning is an important dimension for adult learners it is vital that you end your learning event by ensuring that all are clear about the relevance and application of the material you have been working on.**
This is normally catered for by allowing a group and / or individuals to draw up

some kind of action plan and time-scale for its implementation. As manager you will have a role to play in the implementation of any such plans and you should be a major player in their design.

▶ **Build in mechanisms for ensuring action plans are carried out or reviewed.**
There may be enthusiasm during your learning event for action plans, but this has a nasty habit of dissipating afterwards. Putting dates in diaries, making commitments to meet, agreeing when to review progress – these are all important to the success of a learning event. Ensure you don't overlook this critical learning dimension.

▶ **Implement any post-event evaluation strategy you have.**
On a practical level, follow up on issues such as absenteeism. Consider how, for example, the absence of a group member from the event will impact on any group decision or new commitment. Which other managers need to be involved or consulted as a result of group decisions or action plans?
See also the next section for some further thoughts on this.

In the material above we have tried to offer just a glimpse of some of the practical techniques on which a good facilitator can draw. You will, in time, begin to develop your own, and you may already feel you want to add other items. Although not an exhaustive list, we believe we have included the principal issues, and we hope it will, taken with the earlier material on facilitation, provide you with a firm foundation for becoming an effective facilitator.

Checklist

Question	Notes
Have I anticipated all of the 'befores'?	
Have I arranged and inspected the proposed learning environment?	
Am I clear on all the resources I need and are they on order?	
Do I know what I plan to do to 'kick off' the event effectively?	
If using a Part 2 activity, have I read it through?	
Do I genuinely want to play the role of facilitator?	
Do I know the basic rules of good facilitation and do I feel I can apply them?	
What ideas do I have for ensuring the event leads to clear learning outcomes/action plans?	

5 Evaluation

This is a traditionally neglected phase of the learning process, partly because it is quite difficult to carry out effectively and with the certainty of getting valid results. If you have invested the time and effort in carrying out a TNA, converting the results into learning objectives, designed a group learning event for your team and facilitated it, it surely makes sense to know if your team has met the learning objectives you set. Otherwise, how do you know if that investment has been worth while? You should be interested in the wider context, too – not just looking at whether or not specific learning objectives have been met, but whether or not your overall training programme is being effective.

Most trainers would recognise that there is a hierarchy of evaluation, by which we mean you start with the simple and move to the complex! Let's look at this idea.

The hierarchy can be shown like this:

Evaluation of reaction to the learning event

Evaluation of learning

Evaluation of behaviour change

Evaluation of impact on the business

The top level is the easiest to carry out. You, or the group, or jointly, can undertake a post-event analysis, either by discussing the learning objectives and how far people feel they have been satisfied, or by asking the group to complete a questionnaire immediately after the event.(These questionnaires are often known as 'happiness sheets' since they are normally influenced by good feelings about the event and people are often 'led' into giving favourable responses by the way in which the questionnaires are worded.) At the very least they should give an early indication of any fundamental failings in the event's design but they may not reveal significant minor shortcomings, for participants are usually in a positive, less critical frame of mind at the close of a 'good' event.

The next level down tries to test out what learning has actually taken place. This would show itself in expressed confidence (for example) about new or enhanced skills, claims to having changed attitudes and so on.

The third level looks at to what extent the new skills, attitudes and so on are put into effect and have an impact back at work. This is sometimes called transference of skills.

The final level is determined by such questions as 'Has output risen?, 'Is our level of complaints falling?' and so on.

The problem with evaluations of this kind is that the further down the hierarchy you proceed, the more difficult it is to isolate the learning event as the sole factor. Let's consider our security guard's training once again, taking just one of the learning objectives we identified earlier in this chapter.

Recall the following learning objective: '. . . should be able to apply self-defence skills in an emergency situation where personal danger to the participant would otherwise result'.

We can give the following examples of the four levels of evaluation:

Evaluation of reaction to the learning event

By direct questioning of the security guard participant, ascertain if she or he enjoyed the event and whether or not she or he feels it met the agreed learning objectives. This is usually pursued through such questions as 'What did you want to achieve from coming on this programme?' and 'To what extent do you feel you achieved it?' In the case of the chosen learning objective, the participants presumably came on the course to learn specific techniques, so the question would establish whether they feel that they have, in fact, achieved this. Any major shortcomings with either or both of content and process should emerge at this level.

Evaluation of learning

By direct questioning, ascertain in what way the participant feels they are now better equipped to defend themselves if necessary (assuming they feel this at all). Specific evidence of skills acquisition would be sought out here. For example, at the first level of evaluation, the test is 'Do you feel your learning objectives have been met?' whereas at this level the test is 'Tell us specifically HOW your learning objectives have been met.

This level can be carried out immediately after the event and/or at some later date.

Evaluation of behaviour change

By direct questioning and/or observation of circumstances which allow the learning objectives to be tested (hopefully infrequent in this example) checking to see if the skills are effectively put into practice.

Evaluation of impact on the business

In this example, the evaluation is much more difficult to identify. It may show in terms of greater confidence of the individual (knowing they are less vulnerable) and thus better overall work performance, or it may result in changed attitudes of staff, knowing the security presence is better equipped than it was to resolve unpleasant problems. This may show itself in better motivation through greater comfort at work, lessening of tension and so on.

It would also be appropriate at this level to consider the cost-benefit of your learning event, possibly accounting for its effectiveness through some kind of report to senior management for example.

This example demonstrates an important point about evaluation. It shows the increasing difficulty, as you progress down the hierarchy, of isolating the impact of the learning objective from other factors. Although it's arguable that the security guard's greater self-confidence might contribute to better overall performance, it might equally be due to a good pay rise or a change in supervisor.

Your strategy for evaluation will also be determined by the original source of the TNA, which we referred to in the first section. Achievement of learning objectives which result from, say, a need to change the culture of the business may be more difficult to assess in the learning term than, say, a security guard's self-defence skills, which may result from a lower-level TNA. This will be because cultural change will not be solely the result of training (we earnestly hope) but will result from other major changes within the business, such as organisation, communication technologies, personnel and so on. In these cases training can only be a part of the wider scene (a familiar theme) and is thus much more difficult to assess. Nevertheless, most facilitators of learning would want to evaluate their programmes not just in terms of 'warm feelings' by all after the event (seductive though this may be) and will want to draw up a schedule of post-event analysis.

Kenney and Reid's book (*see* Bibliography) contains a useful section on the methods which can be used to achieve this. It is not our intention here to do more than alert you to the importance of evaluation, both in terms of assessing value for money (investment of money and time) and of determining whether or not your learning event has produced the desired results in the longer term.

Landmark

Question	Notes
What do I understand by the hierarchy of evaulation?	
What proposals are in place for (at the very least) assessing the first three levels?	

2

ACTIVITIES

1 Basic communication skills

Activity 1
• •
ALIENS

Description

This is a light-hearted activity with a serious purpose – to show how important it is to use vocabulary suited to your 'audience'; to give information in small, easily assimilated amounts, and in a logical sequence. The activity takes a tongue-in-cheek look at the English language to help participants recognise the need for clarity of thought and communication.

Aim

To enable participants to be more aware of practical steps in communication and dialogue which can be taken to promote better understanding.

Time

Up to 2 hours (depending on numbers)

Resources

● Subject cards (*see* Trainer notes)
● Visual aids as available – at least a flipchart, paper and markers, means of attaching sheets to wall; if possible flipchart stand and pad, overhead projector, transparencies and markers, chalkboard and chalk, etc.
● Sufficient space for syndicate groups to prepare their presentations – separate seminar rooms if possible

Method

1 Trainer input: to introduce the activity. Many customer complaints about defective products are because the consumer has either misinterpreted or misunderstood working instructions. Interdepartmental jargon can cause confusion. Technical and professional specialists – and, increasingly, man-

agers – use well-understood and accepted forms of language when communicating with each other. However, this frequently results in barriers – intimidating (whether real or perceived) – to those who would wish to understand and relate to such people. Dealing with clients whose first language is not English can create all sorts of difficulties – both in understanding and being understood. Participants may well already have dealings with overseas clients (most of whom, it must be said, have a far greater command of English than we do of foreign languages). However, there will be many occasions when the client or their representative has only very basic English.

This activity will highlight some of these issues and in particular the ambiguities of the English language. It will ask participants to reflect on how communication is structured – logical sequencing – and to think about how to choose appropriate vocabulary to the client's level of understanding.

2 Trainer input: to brief the group on procedure and timing of the activity. The group will be divided into syndicate groups of no more than four. Each syndicate group will be given a card on which is written the subject of a presentation which they will have to give to the whole group after preparation time. The snag is, that during the presentation, the rest of the group, the 'audience', will pretend that they are from another planet, dissimilar to ours (hence the title, 'Aliens'). Although the aliens have a rudimentary knowledge of the English language, they only know basic words and have no idea of technical jargon, will not understand complicated words or phrases, and will have no prior knowledge of concepts perhaps familiar to you and me. For example, an alien would not only be unfamiliar with the word holiday, but the concept of having time off from work and lying on a beach all day, might literally be 'alien' to 'it'.

The audience of aliens is therefore to halt the presentation to ask for clarification whenever a word or concept is mentioned which is likely to be unfamiliar, or where explanations are not logical, or insufficient information has been given for understanding. For example, from the above sentence regarding the holiday, someone might question 'what is a beach?'. The presenters must then explain this to the aliens' satisfaction before continuing. (Rather like explaining something to a small child who constantly asks 'what's this for?' and 'why?').

Syndicate groups will have 30 minutes preparation time. Obviously some presentations will take longer than others, so no time limit will be set, but the trainer may close a presentation at her/his discretion, i.e. if a group gets into a terrible tangle – it has happened – the trainer can decide to let them off the hook. No presentation will be longer than 15 minutes, however.

Syndicate groups can use any visual aids available in the course room. The presentations can be made by one elected member of the syndicate group, or can be a joint effort.

3 Set up syndicate groups and distribute topic cards. If a syndicate group is really unhappy with the selection, or would be unable to give a presentation on the subject allocated, ensure that you have an alternative to offer.

4 If rooms other than the main course room are to be used for preparation, allocate space and set groups to work. This may, of course, be dictated by the number of flipchart stands available, whether or not overhead transparencies are single sheet or on a roll attached to the projector. There may have to be some negotiation over visual aids.

5 Give a time check at 20 minutes. Renegotiate times if necessary.

6 Recall syndicate groups to the main training room. Use any means you wish to select which syndicate group will present first.

7 Remind participants not involved in the presentation that they are to assume a child-like knowledge of vocabulary and concepts, and to query anything that is not clear or logically presented.

You may have to get the ball rolling by intervening yourself until the 'alien' audience get the hang of what's required of them. Questions like 'what's a . . . ?' or 'where do . . . come from?' or 'why does that happen?' Typical words to query are multi-syllabled ones such as 'hibernate'. (An alien might understand the words 'high', 'burn' and 'ate' but the concept created by these three images could well cause confusion!)

8 Let the presentations commence. This activity can generate a lot of laughter, but be sensitive to the needs of the presenters; don't let it get too silly or out of hand! Remember too that it should be a lot easier for the last groups to present once they realise the difficulties the first presenters had and how to overcome these.

9 Thank syndicate groups for their efforts. Lead a discussion on the learning points. First encourage the group to unpack its feelings about the activity itself.

Questions you might use:

- Was that an enjoyable experience while presenting as well as being an 'alien'?
- Why was this? or, Why was it easier to be critical of someone else's efforts?

- Generally, did presenters frequently check with their audience that they had been understood, or did they wait for interruptions?
- Why is it good practice for the presenter of information to check that understanding has taken place?
- What did you learn from the preparation stage?
- Was the presentation easier/more difficult than you expected?
- Were you surprised at some of the questions you were asked?
- Do you think most of the questioning was reasonable?
- Moving outside the activity now, do you think people with only basic English, say, members of a delegation from China, or Tibet, or a country where English is not taught to everyone, would have understood your presentation, or would they have had to query as this group of aliens did?
- What are the messages for technical experts in dealing with non-technical customers?
- What are the messages for anyone having to give instructions or present information?
- What lessons have you learned from this activity?
- Have you been in a learning situation where the tutor (or, if you're really prepared to lay your reputation on the line, the manager) has communicated poorly, given instruction in an illogical sequence, or in large sections, too complicated for you to digest in one go?
- How did that make you feel? What did you do/should you have done about it?
- Can you recall situations where the communicator assumed a basic understanding of the receiver – an understanding which didn't exist (e.g. assuming a member of staff, asked to do a task, knows where the work originated, why it has to be done, and what will happen to it afterwards. Why are statistics needed, for example)?
- Can you identify situations in your working life where you should apply the learning points e.g. when instructing members of your work team, providing information, communicating with people unfamiliar with English, communicating with people unfamiliar with your working practices, jargon and so on?
- In what ways will you apply the learning which has taken place?

10 Close the activity by suggesting that participants could usefully apply the maxim 'Engage brain before opening mouth'!

TRAINER NOTES

Topics for presentations

You will need to reproduce these on cards for distribution:

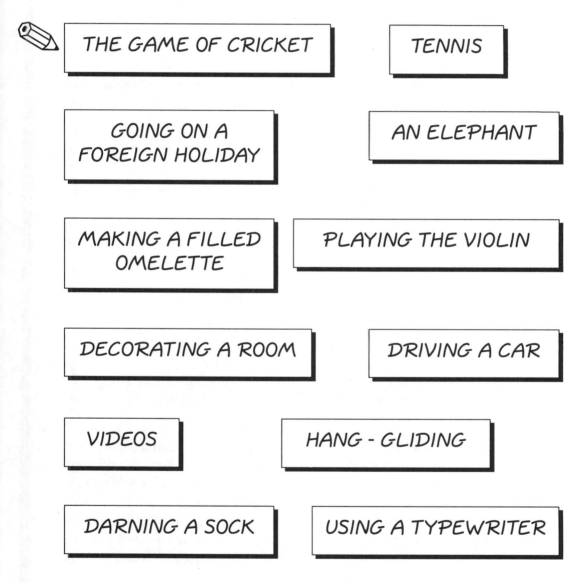

THE GAME OF CRICKET

TENNIS

GOING ON A FOREIGN HOLIDAY

AN ELEPHANT

MAKING A FILLED OMELETTE

PLAYING THE VIOLIN

DECORATING A ROOM

DRIVING A CAR

VIDEOS

HANG - GLIDING

DARNING A SOCK

USING A TYPEWRITER

Activity 2

CAN YOU REPEAT THAT?

Description

An activity to help develop active listening skills.

Aim

Participants should be better equipped to listen to customers/colleagues and to understand their needs. They will practise the skill of repetition to confirm understanding.

Time

30 minutes – 1 hour 30 minutes (depending on number of participants, and whether audio recording is used)

Resources

- A marker pen
- Copy of Trainer notes for each participant if required
- (Optional) An audio recorder

Method

1 Trainer input: to explain the difference between hearing and listening and the importance of active listening for understanding customer needs (*see* Trainer notes).

2 Explain the procedure for the exercise. Participants will sit in a circle. One person, we will call her/him A, will be given the marker pen. A will start speaking about any problem, real or made up, addressing the whole group. Participants should listen carefully to the speaker, because at a time indicated by the trainer, A will be asked to give the marker pen to another in the group – B. B will then repeat what has been said (in the second person, e.g. '. . . you were very annoyed because they had promised to deliver this week') using the same vocabulary as A.

   (Optional) inform the group that the exercise will be recorded to make the feedback session more accurate and productive.

3 Allow the group a few minutes to arrange chairs in a circle and to think of a problem, real or imagined, work or non-work related.

4 Give the marker pen to anyone in the group. (Begin recording.) Start the exercise.

5 At a suitable point (after about 30 seconds) stop A and ask her/him to give the marker to someone else in the group. This person should then repeat, in the second person, what was said, as accurately as possible. In process-ing this step ensure you pick up on examples such as: 'You were cross because they said it would be delivered within a week' would not be an accurate representation of what was said. 'Cross' hasn't the weight of 'very annoyed' and 'this week' is not the same as 'within a week'. When B has repeated what he/she has remembered of A's story, he/she explains their own problem. Again, at a time indicated by the trainer, B will be asked to pass the marker pen to another group member – C – and the process is repeated until every group member has had the chance to repeat another's words, at least once.

   The marker pen should be passed at random with no prior indication to the next recipient, so that each group member listens intently throughout. The pen can be passed to the same person on more than one occasion, so no one can relax having had their go!

6 If recording equipment is not being used, you may wish to take feedback immediately after each exchange. If it is being used, continue the activity until each person has had the opportunity to participate as both speaker and repeater.

7 When everyone has participated, lead a discussion on the activity.

   Questions you might use:

   ● How easy was it for individuals to concentrate?
   ● What caused problems?

   Participants may say that it was the pressure of the situation which caused difficulties in listening accurately, but often listening to others **is** stressful – especially when handling complaints – so active listening is a skill to be practised.

8 If the exercise was recorded, play back the exchanges, noting any differences or free interpretations of originals.

Questions you might use:

- Did listeners sift what was important from supporting material, and repeat just the important?
- Did changes of vocabulary distort meaning? How?
- What are the implications of such distortions for good communication?
- Why is it useful for the listener to reiterate facts/salient points to the speaker?
- How can the skills practised in this exercise – active listening, repeating salient points of another's conversation – be used to advantage in the workplace?
- Give examples of when this skill should be used in the workplace.

9 Issue Trainer notes by way of a handout if appropriate. Close the activity explaining that the exercise involved just one aspect of an important skill – active listening.

TRAINER NOTES

There is a distinction between hearing and listening. Hearing is the passive process whereby we receive sounds. We are all registering sound now on a subconscious level – birdsong, traffic noise, the hum of machinery and so on. Listening is an active process which is under our control. Listening is about interpreting sound and accurately understanding meaning. It is a skill which needs to be practised.

Active and accurate listening is important when taking instructions, attending to customer needs, problems, complaints and so on. One technique which aids accurate listening is to summarise and repeat to the speaker the rudiments of what they have said AS YOU UNDERSTAND IT. This gives them the opportunity to correct you if you have misunderstood, to give additional information if this seems necessary, and to clarify or confirm understanding.

In conversation we all tend to assume that just because we have uttered some words in front of someone else, they will understand and remember what we said. In fact immediately after the average person has listened to someone talk, they can remember only half of what was heard, and the chances are, their own biases and interpretations have distorted that! In everyday conversation it is unlikely that we would be able to repeat another's words verbatim because as we listen, we edit, taking on board the nuances of speech, the body language of the speaker, our own experience of the situation and so on, to arrive at our own understanding of what is being said. Occasional reflective questioning and restating what you heard – 'so you are unhappy about the way we operate the flexi system' – helps both to maintain concentrated active listening, and clarify understanding.

We may be able to restate another's case more accurately for them by using different words to describe a situation, but this needs to be checked for clarification. If someone says 'I was really cross when he said that', it is perhaps necessary to interpret the speaker's perception of the word 'cross'. Did he mean annoyed, very angry, incensed, infuriated, or does the body language convey a different meaning such as 'I was offended . . . ' or 'I was hurt . . . '. You will see that active listening also involves perceptive questioning, both skills which need to be practised.

Activity 3

•••

TELEPHONE TECHNIQUE

Description

An activity in basic communication skills. Participants work through an exercise in a group(s), to discuss what comprises appropriate business telephone etiquette.

Aim

To enable participants to confirm good practice; to evaluate present styles and to agree appropriate telephone technique when both phoning out and receiving calls.

Time

1 hour – 1 hour 30 minutes

Resources

- Copy of Exercise for each participant, plus one extra copy per syndicate group
- (Optional) Copy of Trainer notes/Handout for each participant
- Pens/pencils

Method

1 Trainer input: to explain that, while it would be an insult to everyone's intelligence to suggest they do not know how to use a telephone, it is often skills which we take for granted which encourage lazy habits. How often have we phoned a professional or senior person and received just a curt 'Hello' or 'Yes?' or been in a situation, such as a meeting or interview, when the person in charge has allowed a telephone call to interrupt proceedings.

   This activity is intended as a reminder of good telephone manners, and could show areas where improvements in technique might be made.

2 If necessary, divide participants into smaller syndicate groups – 3 or 4 participants per group would be ideal. If possible, group people together who know each others' work practices or have mutual telephone contact.

3 Issue one copy of the Exercise to each participant plus an extra copy per group, and pens/pencils if required.

4 Explain that groups should discuss each question and annotate only the main exercise sheet. Individuals may wish to keep their own copies as *aides mémoire* after the course. Some of the questions posed will not have definitive answers, but are intended to promote thought and discussion. Allow 30 minutes for completion of the exercise.

5 When group(s) have answered all the questions, invite feedback, asking participants their responses and reasons for them. Emphasise that the questions were intended to promote thought and discussion; there are no definitive answers as each situation will be unique. There are, however, basic good telephone skills which should be followed by everyone in the organisation. Discuss any contentious issues, and if relevant, try to agree appropriate 'standards' for particular work groups or organisations represented. The Trainer notes/Handout gives some discussion points, and could be given as a handout at the end of the session.

6 Close the activity.

EXERCISE – TELEPHONE TECHNIQUE

Discuss the following scenarios. What is good, and what not so good about each?

1 Jack has called Nadil into his office to discuss the projections for the next financial year. They are in deep discussion over the validity of one item of expenditure when the telephone rings. Jack picks up the receiver immediately, puts his hand over the mouthpiece and continues to put his views to Nadil for a few seconds before answering, 'Good morning. Jack Brown speaking'.

NOTES _____

_____

2 'Hello, is that Miss Bishop?'

'Yes, speaking.'

'This is Joan from Glanville Double Glazing; we did some work for you last year didn't we love?'

'Yes, all our windows are now double glazed.'

'Well, we've got an offer dear – for a limited time only for our best customers my love – 40 per cent off any work you need doing, and £50 cash if you recommend us to a friend.'

'Thanks for letting me know – I'll bear it in mind.'

'Do my love. It's an unrepeatable offer and could earn you a few quid for yourself into the bargain. Anyway, thanks for speaking to me my darling; happy new year to you.'

(Transcript of a call actually received by one of the authors – who, incidentally, had never spoken to 'Joan' before.)

NOTES _____

_____

3 'Hello, is that the Spracket Registration Bureau?'

'Yes it is, how can I help you?'

'My name is Henry Jones of Jones and Co., Brinwell. Well, my company has invented a variation on the Nogood Spracket; it's similar in design but has many additional features, so we feel that we might need to register it independently. The thing is, we are a limited company – well it's only myself and a partner really, and we don't want to involve ourselves in any unnecessary expense or bother if our original registration will suffice.'

'Hang on, I'll put you through to someone who can help.'

'Nigel speaking; how can I help?'

'My name is Henry Jones, of Jones and Co., Brinwell. My company has invented a variation on the Nogood Spracket . . . we don't want to involve ourselves in any unnecessary expense or bother if our original registration will suffice.'

'I see, well you really need to talk to Dennis in the adaptation and new invention section; hold the line, I'll see if I can put you through.'

NOTES _____

_____

4 The phone rings. When would the following greetings be appropriate / inappropriate?

a) 'Hallo.'

b) 'Hi there. How's things?'

c) 'Good morning. Jones and Brignell.'

d) 'Jones and Brignell; good morning.'

e) '. . . could you hold the line a minute?'

f) 'Good afternoon Mr Smith; Janet King speaking.'

g) 'Bob Harris – how can I help?'

h) 'Postroom . . .'

Discuss and agree what form of greeting is most appropriate for each member of your group, for external and for internal calls.

NOTES _____

_____

5 John's boss is in a hurry and can't wait to speak to her PA who is attending a medical appointment. She says to him:

'Would you do me a favour? I should have been at Haverlings an hour ago; I've site meetings there all day. I've got to go to Manchester tomorrow because of a crisis at the plant. Book me in at the Rochester tonight and tomorrow night – usual arrangements. Tell them I'll book in around midnight. Bye.'

John phones the Rochester:

'I'm phoning for Mrs Preston of Massey's, Birmingham. Could she have a room for tonight and tomorrow – usual arrangements please?'

'I'm sorry sir, I'm new to the Rochester. What arrangements would these be?'

'Uh, I'm not sure exactly; perhaps I could get back to you with details.'

'I've just checked the bookings sir; we can accommodate Mrs Preston tomorrow – we have a double room free – but tonight we've a Japanese delegation in. We're fully booked I'm afraid.'

'Oh hell! I don't know what to do now.'

'May I suggest I book Mrs Massey in for tomorrow and telephone our sister hotel, the Shrewsbury, to see if they have a room for tonight for her. It's just across town and equally comfortable.'

'Yes OK . . . on second thoughts, no, because I can't get in touch with her today to let her know what's happening . . . Oh blast it . . . sorry . . . I'll have to phone you back.'

Discuss.

NOTES _____

_____

6 Suggest alternatives to the following switchboard operator responses:

'Yes, can I help you?'
'Is that Drewetts?'
'YES. Can I help you?'
'May I speak to John please'
'John who?'
'Sorry, John Jenner.'
'Who's calling?'
'Mr Marworthy.'
'Mr WHO?'
'Marworthy; Sir James Marworthy.'
'And what's it about?'
'It's a personal call.'
'Hold on . . . putting you through.'

NOTES _____

_____

7 How many times should a telephone be allowed to ring before being answered?

NOTES _____

_____

8 A colleague's personal phone is ringing. You know she will be out of the office for two days. What procedure should you follow?

NOTES _____

_____

9 You are trying to connect a caller with another section through the internal telephone system. You know that there is likely to be a delay in this section replying. What procedure should you follow?

NOTES _____

_____

10 List any other bad telephone habits which annoy you.

NOTES _____

_____

TRAINER NOTES / HANDOUT

1 Some of the issues which should have been discussed are whether Jack should have taken any calls having called a meeting with Nadil. This would depend on factors such as whether Jack had a secretary / colleague who could field calls in his absence; whether Jack has a direct line to his office etc., but the basic principle is that formal meetings should not be interrupted by telephone calls.

Generally, it is not acceptable to continue the discourse with Nadil once the receiver has been lifted. Even with a hand over the mouthpiece, it is irritating to the caller to listen to the muffled tail-end of a conversation. An alternative for Jack would be to break off his exchange with Nadil with an 'Excuse me' before accepting the call. In this way Jack can give his full attention to the caller. A 'Sorry about that' to Nadil after the telephone call makes the best of a potentially annoying situation.

Jack's greeting to the caller is fine provided he isn't the first contact the caller has with the organisation, in which case, the company name should have been used rather than Jack's own.

2 Is Joan from Glanville Double Glazing professional in her approach? Many people object to superficial endearments being used. No doubt Joan was trying to appear approachable and friendly, but her technique could prove counter-productive.

What do you think about using abbreviations and slang in business transactions, such as the use of the word 'quid' here?

3 The opening question of this scenario indicates that the receiver of the call to the Spracket Registration Bureau has not adequately identified the organisation. While everyone at Spracket is polite and seemingly helpful, it is the responsibility of the switchboard operator, or the person who first picks up the receiver, to quickly establish what the caller wants and who in the organisation is best equipped to deal with the call. It is extremely annoying, time-consuming and expensive for a caller to be passed from one department or individual to the next, having to relate her/his enquiry in full at each stage.

On the other hand, there will be callers who 'waffle' and who need help in expressing the purpose of their call. Prompting and enquiry will again be necessary in order to connect the caller with the appropriate department in the organisation – e.g. 'Is this a general enquiry, or do you want to place an order?'.

4 a) Unless you are the only one who could possibly be answering that particular phone, this greeting alone is a waste of time, as the response of the
caller is likely to be 'Is that . . . ?' to which you'll have to answer 'Yes . . .',
in other words, three lines of useless (and costly) dialogue. The only time
'Hallo' is warranted is to establish whether you are connected to anyone.

b) Fine if, for example, the switchboard operator announces a caller to
whom you are well known and on friendly / intimate terms. With this
exception, slang and familiarity should be kept out of business calls.

c) d) Either is acceptable. Most books on the subject prefer d) because the
name of the company is the primary interest of the caller. However, it is
important to ensure that the name of the company is enunciated clearly,
as often the first words of the interaction are 'lost' to the caller. An
argument for c) being the preferable approach is that using the
pleasantries first gives the caller's brain a second to 'tune in' and then
register the name of the company accurately.

e) This depends on the circumstances in which these words are used. If in
the middle of a conversation – while one person goes to look for a file, for
example – this is acceptable, although 'will you hold the line *please*' might
be preferable. However, if the caller has just been connected and the first
thing she / he hears are the words 'Could you hold the line a minute' it is
extremely annoying, as the caller is left speaking to a void, not knowing
how long she / he is expected to hold on, or the reason for the delay.

This practice is common with some organisations who feel that a
telephone cannot be left ringing – it must be answered at all costs, even if
the caller is left waiting for minutes while the receptionist, or whoever,
continues to deal with outstanding business. This is not only extremely
irritating for the caller, but costly, and the practice should be avoided.

f) Perfectly acceptable and polite, and Janet King has set the tone – cordial
and approachable – but unless Mr Smith reciprocates by giving his first
name, a subtle definition of status has been created. This may, or may
not be ultimately acceptable to both parties.

g) Fine, provided Bob Harris is not the first contact the caller has with the
organisation, in which case the name of the company and / or department
would be more appropriate. This is a perfectly acceptable response to an
internal call.

h) Generally, this type of call will be internal, so establishing that the caller is
connected with the intended department is quite adequate.

5 What sort of image is John giving of his company, Massey's? Some of the issues discussed should have been what one should do before making business calls, i.e. getting *all* the facts, being prepared to answer questions, to clarify details and so on; to know when and where a superior/colleague may be contacted, or arrange a time she / he will call in for messages.

However one is tempted, should expletives be used during business calls? How might John have handled the call better? What could be learned from the hotel receptionist's approach?

6 One preferable alternative:

'Good morning. Drewetts.'

'Good morning, may I speak to John please?'

'Do you want to speak with Jon Howard or John Jenner?'

'Sorry, John Jenner.'

'Who's speaking please?'

'Mr Marworthy.'

'Would you mind repeating / spelling your name please?'

'Marworthy. Sir James Marworthy.'

'Could you tell me the nature of your call?'

'It's a personal call.'

'Will you hold the line, please, Sir James; I'll try to connect you.'

7 No more than five times. However, please see notes to 4e) above and 10 below.

8 a) Can you or anyone else help?

   b) Can a deputy / another colleague ring them back?

   c) Do they want to leave a message?

   d) If they prefer to ring back, inform them of the time and date of your colleague's return (check with their diary if possible).

If c) is chosen, ensure that the message is clear and includes the name of the person who called, the time and date of the call, purpose of the call, and what follow-up has been agreed.

9 Inform the caller that there may be some delay in replying. Ask them if they mind holding – they may prefer to leave a message for the section to phone them back. If they agree to hold you should make regular contact, apologising for the delay and asking if they wish to continue to hold, at all times ensuring that the caller does not feel that she / he has been forgotten.

10 This list could include items such as operators not announcing a caller – just saying something like 'A call for you' leaving you no option but to take it; or being in a queue – say in a ticket office – where telephone enquiries take preference over personal callers. After all, we're all queuing! In this instance the 'let the telephone ring only five times' rule should not apply.

Another annoyance is hearing papers being shuffled, or the voice of the person you're speaking to becoming muffled as they readjust the position of the receiver under their chin, or the sound of a keyboard being used – all indicators that the person on the other end of the line is doing something else at the same time as talking to you, i.e. they are not giving you their full attention.

Activity 4

QUESTIONING SKILLS

Description

In order to deliver quality service, it is crucial that customer needs are fully understood. When dealing with customer complaints it is essential that all the facts are gathered and fully comprehended. When working as part of a team, communication needs to be open – challenging sometimes – if both individuals and the team are to be fully effective. All of these issues require high quality communication skills. This activity looks at one of these skills, questioning techniques.

Aim

Participants will be able to demonstrate an understanding of various types of question and their application.

Time

Up to 2 hours

Resources

- Copy of Handout – 'Types of question' for each participant
- Copy of Exercise for each participant
- Pens/pencils and notepaper
- (Optional) Audio recorder

Method

1 Trainer input: to explain that the ability to ask suitable questions in order to fully comprehend another's meaning, is one of the key communication skills. Asking appropriate questions to ascertain facts, to clarify understanding and to encourage the other person to give more information/detail is a skill which can be practised. This activity is intended to make participants more aware of the types of question which can be asked, and to recognise what type of question is appropriate/inappropriate in a given situation.

   copy of the Handout – 'Types of question' to each participant and ough each example.

3 If necessary divide the group into smaller groups of between two and four people. Issue a copy of the Exercise to each participant. Instruct groups that they have 15 minutes to match each example with a type of question, using the Handout as a guide. Participants should make rough notes, but not annotate their sheets at this stage.

4 Reconvene the group. Ask for responses to each of the examples (see Trainer notes). The group should reach a consensus on which type of question fits each example and complete the second column on their Exercise sheet accordingly.

5 Lead a brief discussion on the pros and cons of the various questioning techniques for the groups represented, looking at where each type might be appropriate and where certain lines of questioning should be avoided. You could set the discussion in a context, e.g. handling customer complaints, dealing with a grievance, or interviewing a new recruit.

6 (Optional skills practice session). Ask for two volunteers to role-play a situation in front of the group. They could use one of the examples suggested above – handling a customer complaint, dealing with a grievance or interviewing a new member of staff to establish skills, abilities and so on. The rest of the group should observe and listen closely and make notes of the types of question asked. If possible, make an audio recording of the exchange.

7 If appropriate, use the recording to help facilitate discussion. Ask the observers of the exchange to give constructive feedback on questioning techniques.

8 Repeat steps 6 and 7 with different role players as often as time allows, or is felt necessary for learning to be consolidated.

Variation: Practise skills within the small groups, rotating roles so that each participant has the opportunity to practise questioning, to respond to questioning, and to observe and give feedback.

9 Close the activity.

HANDOUT – TYPES OF QUESTION

The ability to ask pertinent questions of the appropriate kind is a key communication skill. It enables you to establish facts, to clarify understanding, to gain more information and so on. It helps the other person to qualify, give detail, express opinions, needs and feelings – to be better understood.

CLOSED questions can be answered by a 'Yes', 'No', or one word response. Consider the following exchange:

'You seem unhappy; am I right?'

'Yes.'

'Is it the work itself that's bothering you?'

'No.'

'Is it the people you are working with then?'

'Sometimes.'

This sort of dialogue could go on for ever with the questioner stabbing in the dark for clues, and the other person answering with monosyllabic responses.

Closed questions are of some value for brevity in establishing facts, e.g. 'You have been part of this team for four days now; is that correct?' or confirming or summarising answers to questions, e.g. 'So you feel a colleague resents your inclusion?'. The disadvantage of closed questions is that they do not encourage the other person to expand on their response, or to give a thoughtful answer. For this reason, closed questions should be used sparingly and selectively and, where possible, followed by a related open question.

OPEN questions do not allow yes/no responses, so encourage more expansive responses. They begin with phrases such as 'In what way. . .' or the words 'Where', 'Who', 'Why', 'When', 'What' or 'How'.

DIRECT questions are open questions requiring an explicit response, e.g. 'Why are you unhappy?'

GENERAL questions are used to ascertain another's understanding of a concept or system, or their perception of a certain issue, e.g. 'What skills do you have which you feel are being undervalued?'

PROBING questions draw out more information from the responder, e.g. 'Why was that?', 'How did that make you feel?'. Probing questions should be used to clarify understanding of information already offered by the other person.

LINKING questions are useful for returning to topics previously just touched upon, or for making smooth transitions from one issue to another, e.g. 'Earlier you mentioned the Stymie system; what other similar systems have you worked with?'

REFLECTIVE questions are used to clarify understanding, and to encourage the other person to say more. The technique requires the questioner to repeat or rephrase the responder's last words with a questioning inflection, e.g. 'You are being misjudged in this?'. If presented in summary form, reflective questioning can move the conversation along, e.g. 'So you're saying that you're unhappy with this lack of communication. In what way could the situation be improved?'

MULTIPLE questions are those which are long, unwieldy and multifaceted. They can confuse both the responder and the person who asked the questions, e.g. 'Hi. How are you? Is John in? Does he know I need to see him about the Glick report? How is his diary looking this morning?' An accurate, but unlikely response would be, 'Hello. Actually I've got a touch of the flu, but thanks for asking. John will be in later today and yes, he does know you need to see him, but his diary is full for the rest of the day I'm afraid.' Far better to ask one, single facet question at a time.

HYPOTHETICAL questions are about issues which didn't happen, or which might never happen. They usually begin with phrases such as 'What would you do if . . .' or 'What would have happened if . . .'. They can be useful in problem-solving activities, but elsewhere could be seen as time-wasting, or patronising.

LOADED questions can put the other person on the defensive. A question such as 'What do you think about the new legislation on . . .' is a loaded question because the responder may not know the questioner's opinion, so is unsure how best to reply/not to offend. A well phrased, loaded question can be useful to test another's ability to think through an issue, e.g. 'The organisation has decided to . . .; what do you see as the advantages and disadvantages of such a ruling?'

LEADING questions, such as 'I think it's disgraceful, don't you?' are inappropriate because the required answer is indicated in the question. Leading questions can be used constructively if structured to check a person's knowledge or attitudes, e.g. 'You wouldn't discriminate against a colleague for that reason would you?'.

EXERCISE

Example   *Type of question*

1 Are you familiar with databases?   _____

2 So you're worried about losing pay?   _____

3 What would have happened if that
   bearing had come loose?   _____

4 I think it's appalling, don't you?   _____

5 In what way could we have been
   more helpful?   _____

6 I expect everyone to work overtime
   on Friday. OK?   _____

7 Are you a good typist?   _____

8 Why did you take that approach?   _____

9 Why did you do that first? Did you
   consult Bob? Didn't you know that
   my work took priority?   _____

10 Earlier you mentioned your workload.
   In what way is this giving you problems?   _____

11 How do you propose to fund the project?   _____

12 Why was that?   _____

13 How does the Frubel system work?   _____

14 Do you smoke?   _____

15 'I retrieved the information from
   bar codes.'
   'Bar codes?'   _____

TRAINER NOTES

With the exception of two, all the examples are OPEN questions in that they require more than a yes/no response. However, they are also examples of hypothetical, leading, probing questions etc. There are no 'right' or 'wrong' answers; there may be overlap; meaning can change with intonation and with different contexts, so the following information should be taken as a loose guide to processing the exercise. Further discussion should be encouraged.

Suggested 'answers'

1 CLOSED question requiring only a yes or no response. This is fine for establishing facts, but needs follow-up, specific questioning to ascertain detail, e.g. what sort of databases; the degree of familiarity, and so on.

2 REFLECTIVE question. Repeating or paraphrasing a person's last words with a questioning inflection can be used to confirm understanding, and/or to suggest that you have not understood / require more information on that point.

3 HYPOTHETICAL question. In this context, possibly a rebuke. As the bearing obviously *hadn't* come loose there is little point in speculating what *might* have happened. Depending on the tone of voice used, this sort of question could spark an argument. Hypothetical questions should be used with care. They can be usefully applied when testing another's problem-solving ability or in group brainstorming sessions.

4 LEADING question. The required answer is indicated in the question. It requires confidence, and good assertion skills to reply in the negative.

5 PROBING question, drawing out more information and detail.

6 LEADING question as 4 above.

7 CLOSED question where only a subjective response is possible. Specific questioning would be more productive, e.g. 'What are your typing speeds?'

8 DIRECT, an open question requiring a direct response.

9 MULTIPLE question, likely to cause misunderstanding and confusion. The responder will possibly be perplexed by this kind of barrage, and is likely to answer only the last question heard.

10 LINKING question, showing that the listener has not lost sight of an important point made earlier. Linking in this way allows another topic to be introduced/reintroduced to the conversation.

11 OPEN, GENERAL question encouraging the responder to give facts, and expand on her / his understanding of an issue.

12 PROBING question used to clarify understanding of information already given.

13 OPEN, GENERAL question, as 11 above.

14 CLOSED question. If said while proffering a packet of cigarettes, a yes or no is all that is required (plus a 'Thanks' of course!). It is a fact-finding question. If, however, this question were asked at interview to an applicant, the question could be seen as LOADED. It can be assumed that some importance is attached to the issue of smoking by the questioner, but the applicant does not know whether the person asking the question favours a smoker, or whether preference would be given to applications from non-smokers. The applicant is in a 'Catch 22' situation.

15 REFLECTIVE question, as 2 above.

Activity 5

••

WRITE IT RIGHT

Description

An activity which looks at written communication skills.

Aim

Participants will analyse an example of poor letter writing and discuss and agree good practice.

Time

1 hour

Resources

- Copy of Exercise – 'Example of poor letter writing' for each participant
- Copy of Trainer notes/Handout for each participant
- Notepaper, pencils/pens

Method

1 Trainer input: to explain that there is no one correct way to write business letters, but there are some general principles which should be followed, not the least of which is that plain, simple, concise language is called for. Business does not need a special language of its own. Words and phrases in common usage fulfil all the needs of industry.

Unless technical terms and expressions are called for, due to the nature of the business, always try to use the shortest word which expresses the meaning; usually they are easier to spell and to understand. Similarly, the shorter the sentence, the easier it is to follow. Use punctuation to aid understanding, but use it carefully as incorrect punctuation may change the meaning you intend.

Plan the letter well so that you know what you are going to say, how you are going to say it, and how you are going to order it – what is a logical sequence? If the letter is a reply, make sure that you know exactly what you have been asked, and that you have all the necessary facts to respond appropriately.

2   Instruct participants that they will work in pairs/triads to analyse an example of a poor business letter (it is far easier to criticise someone else's work than to construct a good example of your own).

3   Divide group into pairs/triads and issue a copy of the Exercise to each participant, plus notepaper, pens and pencils if required.

4   Participants have 30 minutes to find the deliberate errors – there are around 30, so anyone who finds 20 is doing well.

5   Back in the main group, go through the letter line by line, teasing out the learning by discussing errors and encouraging appropriate alternatives.

6   (Optional) In order to reinforce the learning (as opposed to enjoying the process of pulling apart a bad letter) it would be a good idea to suggest that participants might draft a letter which conforms to good practice. This is best done on a topic of relevance to each individual and it requires time. The best way of arranging this would be to ask for drafts in time for the next meeting of the group. These can then be copied and distributed. Group criticisms can be called for, but do ensure that there is positive criticism (teasing out the good points) as well as negative.

7   (Optional) Issue Trainer notes/Handout.

8   Close the activity.

EXERCISE – EXAMPLE OF POOR LETTER WRITING

This is an example of bad business correspondence. What is wrong with it?
Using the line numbers, list specific errors in sequence.

1	'Dunromin'
2	Hart Close
3	Newtonland
4	Stropshire

5

6 Dear Sir,

7

8 I acknowledge reciept of your letter of the 21st inst in connection with
9 our order's for clonium welding and your problems with our specs.
10 I'm glad that a firm timetable in relation to the work to be undertaken
11 can now be drawn up, and that you can recommence with our orders
12 again. Would you kindly proceed with delivery at your earliest
13 convenience.

14

15 Re. your following paragraph. This has been put into the hands of
16 our accounts section as it is their responsibility to pay suppliers for
17 services rendered. I am sorry about the misunderstanding, and delay,
18 doubtless due to the papers being unfortunately mislaid, during filing.

19

20 You suggest we could meet to fully examine the technical problems
21 consequent upon modification and inurement to standardisation.
22 There are a number of alternatives. I'm visiting your plant next week,
23 and could see you then, or you could give me a call arrange a
24 meeting here. Its up to you: whatever suits you best.

25

26 Assuring you of our best attention at all times.

27

28 Yours sincerely,

29

30

31 Kevin Twit
32 for Chief Engineer

33

34

35 Mr John Smith Esq
36 (Production Manager)
37 Stannards & Co
38 Fortknightly
39 Stropshire

TRAINER NOTES

There are well over 20 deliberate mistakes. Although this is an exceptionally bad letter, many of the mistakes listed are common errors.

The address

As Kevin has chosen to use his home address, early reference should have been made to the company he represents. He didn't include a postal code; this could lead to a postal delay.

Telephone number

Not included

The date

There isn't one.

Line 6

Impersonal. When a person's name is known, it should be used – Dear Mr Smith, or Dear John, if on first name terms. (In some instances organisations require letters to be addressed to them rather than to individuals, in which case Dear Sirs, would be appropriate.)

Line 8

Spelling error – receipt. Always check letters for style, construction and spelling before sending out.

Line 8

21st inst – as the letter hasn't been dated, this phrase is meaningless. Abbreviations such as 'inst' are antiquated anyway; much better to write 'Thank you for your letter of 21st January.'

Line 9

Apostrophe used incorrectly to form a plural – should be 'orders'.

Line 9

specs – abbreviations are not appropriate in formal writing. In this context, John

Smith would probably realise that Kevin meant 'specifications' and was not, in fact, referring to his 'spectacles', 'spectators' or to 'speculations'.

Line 10

I'm – it is not strictly correct to use contractions in formal letter writing.

Line 10

in relation to – an unnecessary phrase. The preposition 'for' is more suitable. Do not use a stereotyped phrase to express a meaning which can be conveyed by a single word.

Line 11–12

recommence with our orders again – the 'again' is superfluous; the whole construction unwieldy.

Lines 12–13

Needless accumulation of words. Better to write 'Please start delivery again as soon as possible.'

Line 15

Re. your following paragraph. – this is not a sentence. Either a verb should be included or a semicolon used. Re. is a colloquialism for 'regarding' and is obviously an abbreviation so should be avoided. Its formal meaning, in legal parlance, is 'in the matter of'. Generally, short words are easier to understand and to spell, so 'next' might be preferable to 'following'. However, a reference to the *subject* of the paragraph would have been better still.

Lines 15–18

It is unprofessional to pass the buck, or blame other sections for errors.

Lines 17–18

Overuse of the comma.

Line 20

to fully examine – this is a split infinitive. It should be 'to examine fully'. Though, today, we are more lax about grammar, it is best to avoid placing adverbs between two parts of the verb in this way.

Lines 20–21

Unnecessary verbiage! It is a mistaken notion that long, impressive sounding words and roundabout phrases indicate an educated mind, or a writer of high status. Trying to impress in this way often leads to using words incorrectly thus totally defeating the object!

Line 22

There are a number of alternatives – the subject of a sentence must agree in number with its verb; that is both must be singular or both must be plural. Here the subject is 'number' (singular) so the sentence should read 'There *is* (singular) a number of alternatives.' In this context, the word 'alternatives' is incorrectly used. There can be only two alternatives (dictionary definition 'of two things' 'mutually exclusive', 'either / or') beyond that number, they become options.

Lines 23–24

Too passive. When, exactly, is Kevin visiting John Smith's plant? Where is 'here' – Kevin's home address, or his place of work?

Line 23

a call arrange a meeting here – check for missing words.

Line 24

Its – should be 'It's'. There is often confusion between abbreviations for 'it is' which should have an apostrophe, and 'its' meaning belonging to it, which shouldn't have the apostrophe. Misuse of a colon. A semicolon would be best here as it provides a longer pause than a comma, and permits the joining of short related thoughts. The colon is very occasionally used to indicate a more emphatic pause than a semicolon, but is used mainly to introduce a list.

Line 26

Omit entirely. Never end a letter with a stereotyped or meaningless formula such as 'We beg to remain' or 'Awaiting a favourable reply' or 'Awaiting the favour of your further advice'. Some letters may need a final paragraph to sum up, or to indicate action – 'I shall phone you or your secretary early next week to see when a meeting might be arranged' – but if the main letter has followed a logical sequence, a final paragraph is often superfluous.

Line 28

'Yours faithfully' should be used after 'Dear Sir'; 'Yours sincerely' only after personal salutations such as 'Dear Mr Smith' or 'Dear John'.

Lines 35–39

Addressee should appear first, not last. This name and address should appear in the top left-hand corner of the page.

Line 35

Either John Smith Esq, Mr John Smith, or Mr J Smith, but not 'Mr' followed by 'Esq'.

Line 36

Bracketing the title in this way is demeaning. Brackets *could* be acceptable if used to differentiate between, say, areas of expertise – Director (Finance).

2 Assertion skills

Activity 6

....

KEEP YOUR COOL

Description

Participants will practise giving professional responses to potentially stressful situations – giving and receiving criticism, dealing with complaints, calming the angry customer and so on.

NB This activity could usefully be preceded by those on listening and questioning skills.

Aim

To enable participants to: improve communication skills; recognise the needs of others while not undermining their own; handle difficult or highly charged situations in an unemotional and constructive way.

Time

2 hours

Resources

- Copy of Handout – 'Keep your cool' for every participant
- Notepaper, pens/pencils
- 'Props' as required for individual skills practice

Method

1 Trainer input: to explain the purpose and procedure of the activity. One of the most demanding aspects of customer care is dealing with difficult cases – the angry complainant; the people in the other department who seem determined to make your life as complicated as possible; the unreasonable demands from management; being criticised, whether or not that criticism is justified, and so on. It is easy to get angry or demoralised, to meet aggres-

sion with aggression, to resort to sarcasm or to become defensive – the list of unproductive reactions is endless. It is not so easy to stay calm, and help develop a positive and constructive dialogue where problems can be identified, feelings expressed, solutions discussed and needs met.

This activity offers some advice and gives the opportunity to practise skills in a safe and supportive environment. After discussing some methods for handling difficult cases, participants will work in groups of three or four, practising these techniques.

2 Issue and discuss Handout – 'Keep your cool'. Allow sufficient time for participants to read the Handout. (NB This is quite a long document and you may need to be especially alert to any participants who may have problems with reading. It's important that the contents of the Handout have been absorbed before proceeding so follow any of the suggestions in the chapter on facilitation skills if necessary). Ask for observations and take questions.

Questions you might use:

- Why is it important to assess what has not been said as well as listening and understanding the words spoken? (*To try and give a holistic approach to the issue rather than just dealing with the symptoms.*)

- Why is it important to use questioning skills? (*Using the appropriate type of question to get the full picture – to ascertain facts and allow the other person to add relevant detail.*)

- What is likely to happen if you retaliate to another's anger with defensiveness . . . or annoyance . . . or a 'couldn't care less' attitude? (*The anger will probably escalate, the problem may remain unresolved; there could be loss of goodwill.*)

- In connection with body language, what is meant by 'open stance'? (*A relaxed – but not laid back – appearance. The avoidance of 'crossing' gestures – folded arms etc., or of a passive look – hanging head, lowered eyes, despondent demeanour*).

- Which of the five suggestions for handling criticism would you find most hard to do?

- Why is it often difficult to respond positively to criticism?

- What are the benefits of using the suggested methods of handling criticism?

Point out that the techniques suggested in the Handout need a lot of practice. The rest of the activity will give participants the opportunity to begin that practice in a supportive and non-threatening environment.

3 Divide group into syndicate groups of three or four. Explain that each person should think of a real work situation involving another person, where the communication and/or outcome was felt to be unsatisfactory. The incident should not be too complex or emotionally charged. It can be complaint handling, dealing with an angry or abusive customer, colleague, boss etc., coping with criticism, refusing a request – any situation which has caused difficulty.

Allow ten minutes thinking time. Participants can chat within their groups and make notes if they wish.

4 Trainer input: to explain that participants will take it in turns to recount their incident to others in the group, giving as accurate a description as possible of the interaction: actual words used; tone of voice; body language and so on.

With a partner, participants will re-enact the incident as accurately as possible. (Were you standing or sitting originally? Would 'props' help recreate the situation?) The other group member(s) should observe closely.

Groups will then discuss the interaction and suggest ways the situation might have been handled differently to arrive at a mutually satisfactory conclusion.

The two will then replay the incident trying out behaviours suggested in the Handout, and using suggestions from the group.

In total, these stages should last no longer than 20 minutes per person.

These stages then repeat so that each participant has re-enacted her/his own incident, received constructive feedback from colleagues, and has had the opportunity to replay, practising improved communication skills.

5 Set groups to work. Circulate to ensure that no individual's skills practice is going on too long. It is important that every participant has the chance to rehearse and repeat their interaction.

6 Reconvene the main group to discuss learning points.

Questions you might use:

- When you recreated your incident, did you feel similar emotions? Which were the same; which different, and why? Can you analyse these reactions now and realise why you felt that way? How might you deal with these feelings in future?

- Has the activity helped you to see your incident from others' perspectives?

- In what way was the small group discussion helpful?

- How did you feel about the replay of the incident? What went well? What didn't go so well? Why?

- What changes in behavioural style would help in future similar situations?

7 Close the activity by encouraging participants to continue to practise techniques for handling difficult situations and to prepare action plans for the future.

HANDOUT – KEEP YOUR COOL

Dealing with difficult people or demanding situations requires solid base–line communication skills.

Listening Skills: the ability to listen, *actively,* to the other person, picking up nuances from tone of voice, body language and so on – 'listening' to what has *not* been said as well as the words spoken. Letting the angry person 'let off steam' before trying to defuse the situation.

Questioning skills: being able to ask appropriate questions to establish facts and gain more information so that together you can fully define the problem, e.g. 'When did this happen?', 'How is that a problem?', 'Which one specifically?', 'Could you tell me more about . . .?'

Verbal skills: being able to acknowledge that you've heard and understood the other person (this doesn't mean saying 'I know how you feel'. Unless you can get into the skin of that person, you can't know *exactly* how they feel!). Using appropriate language without patronising, antagonising – or grovelling. Summarising what you have heard to clarify understanding. Asking if there is anything else that is bothering the other person – you are inviting more criticism, but best to get all problems out into the open.

Non-verbal skills: maintaining good eye contact; using appropriate noises to encourage the other person to continue speaking, and to let them know you are paying attention etc.; making sure that your body language matches what you are saying (show an 'open' stance to convey composure). Don't give your true feelings away, however annoyed you might feel (don't grind your teeth, or tap your foot, or drum your fingers, etc. to show impatience). However you feel inside, maintain an air of composure.

You will also need to have **problem-solving skills**. Try to get an *accurate, objective* picture of the complaint or criticism, not what you *think* is meant, intended or hinted at. Work with the other person to establish a clear definition of the problem. This is the most important step towards putting things right.

If there has been an error – or if criticism of you, your department or organisation is shown to be justified – it is important to avoid a defensive reaction. There are techniques for dealing with this:

1 Acknowledge the criticism without necessarily agreeing with it. Saying something like 'That's possibly true' recognises their viewpoint without saying that they are right.

2 Accept that there might be room for improvement. 'Yes, we might consider doing it that way' or 'That's an interesting approach; I might consider that'

isn't complying with the complaint or criticism, but gives the other credit for a useful idea (which you might or might not pursue).

3 Recognise when feelings and emotions are high, 'I can see that you're very annoyed; in your shoes I would be too' – then set about putting things right.

4 Admit responsibility for genuine errors 'Yes, you are right; that shouldn't have left the workshop in that condition' – then set about putting things right.

5 If the complaint or criticism is unjustified, acknowledge that you have understood the other person's viewpoint, 'I can see why you think that' but refute the criticism, adding a phrase such as 'On the other hand . . .' or 'However, from my point of view . . .'

Finally, when all facts have been gathered and communication is on an adult / adult basis, i.e. emotions have cooled and both are being rational, ask for a solution 'How would you like to pursue this?', 'What would you like done about it?' 'Would you happy if we . . .?' If appropriate, suggest a solution or tell the other person what you intend to do about the complaint or criticism. Make sure they understand and agree.

Activity 7

EMPATHY

Description

Looks at areas of disagreement, tension, conflict and so on experienced by participants as the result of either having change imposed on them, or of having to be the instigators of change in the workplace. Participants will look at the values – theirs and the other party's – which led to friction, and discuss ways in which a 'win-win' situation might have been achieved. Suitable for most participants, but it would be particularly useful for supervisors/team leaders.

Aim

To develop analytical skills as a tool to understanding other people's perspectives in order to avoid, or at least minimise, common negative results of change.

Time

1–2 hours

Resources

- Space for groups of 3–5 people to talk privately
- Copy of Exercise – Sheet A for each participant
- Copy of Exercise – Sheet B for each participant
- Pencil/pen for each participant

Method

1 Trainer input: to introduce the activity. Generally, people resent and resist change unless it is introduced with sensitivity, or it is seen to be personally beneficial. The 'what's in it for me?' syndrome still prevails. There will have been times in the past when everyone can recall feeling, at best put out, at worst aggressive and hostile when informed of a decision to upset the *status quo*. Usually that aggression is taken out on the person who has to implement the decision to change, whether or not she/he is responsible for that decision – 'shoot the messenger'!

In any potential conflict situation, it is important to try to understand the other person's position, and to respect their values, however much these values may differ from our own. This activity asks participants, with the help of colleagues, to look at situations which they may have found difficult to cope with in the past, to empathise with the probable value position of the 'opponent(s)' in each case, and to look at ways in which an acknowledgement of the validity of values different from our own could help the management of change in the future.

2 Explain procedures and timings. Participants will be issued with Exercise – Sheet A and asked to think of a situation in the recent or distant past where change initially caused some difficulty. The situation could either be where a change was asked of the individual, or where participants were responsible for introducing change which affected others. There are eight headings – areas which are often affected by change in the workplace. Participants should give examples from as many areas as possible in the time allowed – up to 30 minutes.

After the allocated time participants will be issued with Exercise – Sheet B on which they will summarise the situations identified, and complete the grid as directed. Another 15–20 minutes will be allowed for this.

Participants will then be divided into syndicate groups to discuss the content of each person's sheet. Times for this discussion can be negotiated, but will be approximately 45 minutes.

3 Issue Exercise – Sheet A. Set participants to work. Allow 20 minutes initially for participants to complete the form; renegotiate times if necessary. Circulate to ensure that participants are coping with the task.

4 After the allocated time, issue Exercise – Sheet B, reminding participants that they have 20 minutes to complete the grid. Some people may have had difficulty identifying (or admitting to) situations which have caused friction in all of the areas listed. This is quite acceptable provided they have one or two situations to discuss when it comes to group work.

5 Divide the group into syndicate groups, ensuring that each group has enough space to discuss the issues arising without being overheard by another. This could involve the use of additional rooms if these are available.

6 Inform syndicate groups that they have 45 minutes to look at the situations recorded by each person, and to offer constructive comment on how a 'win-win' situation could have been achieved, alternative approaches which could be adopted in future and so on. The purpose of this discussion is not for participants to commiserate with each other on their unhappy lots! It is to be constructive in further clarifying the two positions (their colleagues', and the other person's in each case), to help individuals identify and empathise with those whose values may be different, and by looking at the

situations from an outsider's perspective, to offer constructive help on how similar situations occurring in the future might be handled.

7 After the allocated time, reassemble the group for a plenary session to share any useful advice resulting from syndicate group discussions. Participants may not wish to share their discussions with the total group, but explain that if anything really useful emerged, it would be good to share it. Or if anything was unresolved in syndicate groups, or individuals feel they would benefit from the advice of the total group, these issues could also be raised here.

8 Ensure that the session closes on a positive note.

Questions you might use:

- What have you learned from this activity?
- What will change as a result of this learning?

EXERCISE – SHEET A

Identify, in the spaces below, situations from your recent or distant past where change has caused you stress or tension, or resulted in friction and conflict with another person. This could be as the result of change being imposed on you, or from you having to be the instigator of change which affected others.

To help you, examples of areas to consider are listed under each heading. Try to think of just one example for each of the eight headings.

MONEY (Salaries, departmental resourcing, bonuses, overtime etc.)

_____

STAFFING (Natural wastage, redundancies, replacements, recruitment etc.)

_____

SYSTEMS (Technology, decentralisation, job redesign etc.)

_____

EQUIPMENT (Computers, telephones, seating, desks, lighting etc.)

_____

STANDARDS (More output, lowered standards, calibre of staff etc.)

_____

TERMS AND CONDITIONS (Hours, holidays, welfare, perks – cars, medical insurance etc.)

_____

WORKING PRACTICES (Production methods, teamwork, shift work etc.)

_____

WORKING ENVIRONMENT (Open plan offices, lighting, ventilation, noise etc.)

_____

EXERCISE – SHEET B

Summarise the situations you have just listed, and complete the following grid, attempting to state not only your perspective, but putting yourself into the other person's shoes, trying to judge their position on the issue.

The situation: what and with whom	My position	Their position
Money		
Staffing		
Systems		
Equipment		
Standards		
Terms and conditions		
Working practices		
Working environment		

Activity 8
....
PLAN FOR PROGRESS

Description

This activity is designed to follow 'Perspectives'. Although it can be run as a separate exercise, it reinforces the learning which has taken place during the previous Activity by relating the issues raised to participants' own working situations. 'Plan for progress' uses the formats suggested by 'Perspectives' to plan meetings where a change of attitude or behaviour is required of others.

Aim

To assist participants to understand why face-to-face meetings to discuss change can go wrong and to offer the opportunity to practise different approaches which may help avoid common 'blockages' to effective dialogue.

Time

2 hours

Resources

- Space for pairs to work with a degree of privacy (for discussion and role-play)
- Copy of Exercise for each participant
- Copy of Handout – 'Plan for progress' for each participant
- Pen/pencil for each participant

Method

1 Trainer input: to explain that this activity will give everyone the opportunity to analyse either:

- a situation in the past where a meeting with a colleague, requiring that person to change their attitude or behaviour, has been less than successful, or

- a current situation where such a meeting is called for.

Ten minutes will be allowed for this part of the activity. Working in pairs, participants will be required to share this information with their partner only – they do not have to divulge their particular situation to the trainer or to the total group if they do not wish to do so.

With their partner, participants will then work through the situation from their own viewpoint under the headings, *What I want, What I feel,* and *My expectations.* Together, they will then try to assess what the other person's goals, feelings and needs, and expectations might be – to look at the situation from the other person's perspective, in other words. This will take about 30 minutes.

Finally, participants will have the opportunity to re-enact and/or rehearse their own situation with their partner. The trainer can offer assistance and advice if required, but partners can pursue the exercise alone if this is more helpful to them. They will not be required to 'perform' in front of the whole group. The role plays will take another 15–30 minutes.

2 Divide group into pairs. If there is an odd number of participants, there will have to be one triad.

3 Issue a copy of the exercise and a pen/pencil to each participant. Explain that time checks will be given so that participants know when to move on to different parts of the activity.

4 Get participants to think of a past or present situation they wish to analyse, and to paraphrase this at the top of their sheets in section A. Allow ten minutes for this. If any participant is having real difficulties either recalling a previous unsuccessful attempt to adapt someone's attitude or behaviour, or recognising a situation where this might occur in the future at their place of work, offer the following hypothetical situation as a suggestion.

A new person has joined your section, recruited by personnel. They have many years' experience of your type of work, but working for a different organisation from which they were made redundant. They insist on doing things their way, saying that their old firm's methods are far superior to yours. Their style of working is incompatible with everyone else's in your section, and is causing hold-ups in production, and resentment from other members of your team.

5 Allow another ten minutes for participants to share the chosen situation with their colleague. Participants should 'put meat on the bones' of their situation in order that their partner has a fair idea of the background and the problems involved.

6 Instruct participants to complete part B of their forms. A time check will be given after 20 minutes. Participants should do this individually without consulting their partner. In the left-hand column, under *WHAT I*

WANT should be listed objective goals, like 'I want him to be more courteous to customers' or 'I want to be sure she gets the message this time'. Under *WHAT I FEEL* should be listed participant's emotional needs, such as 'I feel she always gets away with things' or 'I am really angry at myself' or 'Scenes upset me'. Under *MY EXPECTATIONS* list what you really expected of the meeting, or expect will happen when you have the meeting if it is yet to happen, such as: 'I wanted an adult to adult conversation, but ended up shouting at him' or 'She'll get tearful, so I'll back down again' or 'He'll come up with all sorts of reasons why my idea won't work'.

Participants should then try to put themselves in the shoes of the other person and complete the right-hand side of the grid – what their goals, needs and expectations are likely to be.

7 Circulate around the group, checking that participants are keeping their observations specific and objective. Check progress after 20 minutes. Renegotiate times if necessary, but halt this part of the activity after 30 minutes.

8 Instruct participants to swap forms and to complete part C using their own perceptions of their partner's situation. Allow about ten minutes for this. Participants should put themselves in the shoes of the person who was, or is going to be, on the receiving end of their partner's communication. If *you* were, say, John, Carla or Ahmed, (or whoever) what do you think your goals, needs, feelings and expectations would be in the given situation?

9 Instruct pairs to swap sheets again, and discuss discrepancies between their own observations about the other party's needs and so on, and their partner's thoughts on the issue. It is very likely that another person will be able to project a dimension on the situation not previously considered by the 'owner' of the problem. The feasibility of these perceptions can be analysed, and different approaches to the problem discussed.

10 Get participants to act out their situations with their partners. You might give one or two guidelines as to appropriate approaches to such meetings, for example:

- always hold such meetings in private, away from open offices
- think about the timing of such meetings – not just as the other person is thinking of going home or off on holiday.

Allow 15–30 minutes for this. The role plays should conform to the situation as perceived by the 'owner' and also from the different angle as perceived by the partner to give participants the chance to practise different approaches to various responses.

Remind the 'owner' in each situation that they should:

- have clear objectives – what do they want to achieve by this meeting?
- state their case concisely and firmly
- allow the other person to state their case
- listen to the other person's viewpoint, and take this into consideration
- be specific, and criticise the behaviour, or the action not the person, i.e. 'the report was late, and had several errors in it – why was this?' not 'you're careless; you're slipshod, and you never get your reports in on time'.

11 When participants have gained all they can from role-playing, reassemble the whole group for a plenary discussion of the activity.

Questions you might use:

- How useful was it to analyse the problem from both viewpoints?
- It is usually obvious that both protagonists in these kinds of conversations see the issues solely from their own point of view. How useful is it to use this suggested format in planning meetings where a change of attitude or behaviour is required?
- Were there many differences between the 'owner's' perceptions of the other's viewpoint, and their partner's views on how they would feel if they were on the receiving end of the conversation?
- How helpful was it to see the problem from another, outsider's perspective?
- Did the role-playing produce any surprises?
- Did anyone use humour as a method of relieving the tension of the interview?
- How successful was this?
- Do you think that by behaving differently from what is expected of you, e.g. using humour rather than aggression, could work to your advantage?
- Have you considered that the other person might behave differently from the stereotypical behaviour you have imagined from them – especially if you don't conform to what they expect?

- What have individuals learned from this activity?
- Do you foresee any problems in implementing this format in the workplace?
- What are the benefits of using a format similar to this in the workplace?

12 Issue Handout – 'Plan for progress'.

13 Close the activity.

EXERCISE

 A Summarise either a situation which did not go as well as you would have liked, or an encounter which you intend to have with a colleague, which involved, or will involve, a conversation which should result in a change of their behaviour or attitude.

_____

_____

_____

 B

WHAT I WANT	WHAT .... WANTS
WHAT I NEED	WHAT .... NEEDS
MY EXPECTATIONS	.... 'S EXPECTATIONS

C (*To be completed by your partner*)

You now know a little about your colleague's situation, what went wrong the last time, or what blockages she / he is likely to encounter when having a conversation about a desired change of behaviour or attitude with the colleague.

Try to put yourself in the colleague's shoes. What would you be feeling, expecting, or wanting from the meeting? Please enter your views below.

IF I WERE .... I WOULD WANT:

IF I WERE .... I WOULD FEEL:

IF I WERE .... MY EXPECTATIONS OF THE MEETING
WOULD BE:

HANDOUT – PLAN FOR PROGRESS

Some tips on your approach

1 Use the format suggested: first write down your objectives, needs, feelings, and expectations of the meeting.

2 Now try to establish how the other individual might be feeling about the meeting, by using your grasp of human nature in general, your knowledge of the person, by observation, and by empathy. List these assumptions under similar headings to those above.

3 Consider ways you might alter the expected course of events by planning a different approach.

At the meeting:

4 Know what you want to achieve, and don't close the meeting until this, or a mutually acceptable alternative is reached.

5 Try to preface negative feedback with something positive. When offering constructive criticism, it can really help the receiver to hear first what is good about their work or behaviour. They will then more readily accept any negative feedback.

6 Allow the other person to state their case, and really listen to their point of view. Take this into consideration in any decision about future action.

7 Be specific. 'That report was awful' is not only dreadful to hear, but hard to accept because no details of how or why it was awful are offered. Specific feedback gives more opportunity for learning.

8 Criticise the behaviour, not the person. 'You're just careless' is hurtful, and not strictly accurate. The particular piece of work may have shown careless-ness, but the person may not *always* be careless in *every* aspect of her/his life.

9 Discuss behaviour which can be changed, and offer helpful alternatives. For example, 'It would help me if you let me know immediately you begin to have difficulties with . . . so that we can sort things out before it becomes a major crisis' or 'The fact that you remain at your desk when people come to reception seems unwelcoming. If you walked to the reception area, and dealt with enquiries there, it would give a better impression of the office's helpfulness and efficiency'.

10 To maintain a good relationship during and after the meeting, show the other person genuine respect and empathy. Let them know that they are valued individuals and that you want to help. Share *your* feelings when appropriate. Reassure them about confidentiality.

Activity 9

• •

SORT 'EM OUT!

Description

This activity is one of the simplest in the book – but it is without doubt the riskiest! Please do read carefully the Trainer notes at the end of this activity before you decide whether or not to use it.

It is especially useful in the following circumstances:

• where real-life teams are having to deal with conflict

• where participants are developing strong factional tendencies or animosity towards each other.

Aim

To expose personal and/or factional conflict in order that it may be addressed directly.

Time

Between 30 minutes and 1 hour

Resources

• Wristwatch for timekeeping purposes

Method

1 Make your decision that the activity is necessary. This could result from advance knowledge of the group and an assessment that this activity could be useful or from a need which develops, and which must be dealt with, during a programme.

2 Tell the group that you are going to 'change gear' and undertake a different kind of activity. It's almost certainly best not to explain what this activity is about in advance.

3 Form the group into a circle. Next, 'squeeze' the circle(s) so that it consists of two lines of participants, facing each other. (Squeezing the circle eliminates the choosing of partners by participants). Each participant on one side of the line then has no more than one minute to tell his or her partner

opposite the following:

- one thing they like about that person
- one thing they have difficulty with about that person
- another thing they like about that person.

During this phase, the 'listener' is strictly bound to listen and not to comment, argue, defend – or, indeed, say anything at all. After one minute the roles swap. Ensure that the timing is rigidly managed – no more than two minutes altogether, and that listeners stick to listening! Equally, though, don't (assuming you are their manager) eavesdrop.

The idea behind this structured approach is that it allows a number of problems and conflicts to surface. The knowledge that the listener must try to listen (and won't be allowed to interrupt), together with the 'sandwiching' of negative feedback within positive feedback, can be very reassuring and can encourage openness.

4 After the first two minutes, the line moves 'sideways' so that completely new pairs are formed. Repeat step two until the original positions are reached.

5 Allow a short interval – five minutes – for tea, coffee or a natural break. This is to allow people time to reflect.

6 Reconvene the group. Ask if anyone wants to say anything in general terms about anything they have learned during this activity.

Allow up to 30 minutes if a discussion gets going. Facilitate this, drawing out any points of general application, especially if they contribute to the processes of team development. It might be, for example, that people want to comment on how useful it was to be able to express feelings openly for the first time, or on the difficulty of giving/receiving negative feedback. However, don't force the issue – move on quickly to the next step if no one wants to contribute. **There must be no discussion of individual grievances during this phase**.

7 Draw conclusions which identify how people deal with conflict. Discuss with the group if there are any learning points which might be translated into action points for the future. Allow 15 minutes for this.

Questions you might use:

- How easy is it to fail to take into account people's fears and anxieties in a team situation?

- How can misunderstandings occur and how can they be avoided?
- How far does personality influence how people react to situations (e.g. 'I'll do it, but only because I like her').
- Is conflict always expressed openly? If not, why not?
- What contributes to group/team mistrust? (e.g. imposed change, new team members/leaders, feelings about others' performance).
- What are the learning points that can be drawn on in order to minimise conflict/factionalism in future?

8 Close the activity.

TRAINER NOTES

The risks in running this activity should be obvious. We have only included the activity in this book at all on the assumption that it will be facilitated **by an experienced manager or supervisor**.

As such you should satisfy yourself on the following points before you contemplate using the activity:

● Is my group mature enough, both as a group and in terms of the individuals within it, to handle this activity in an adult fashion?

● Are there issues I know about and which I, as manager, should deal with before they 'explode' in an activity such as this?

● What am I prepared to do, both during and after this activity, to address unresolved grievances and personal animosities which might surprise me and others during this activity? Is my reputation such that I can act as 'honest broker' if conflicts emerge which cannot be resolved between the two people concerned?

● Do I feel confident enough, as a manager, to deal with interpersonal difficulties which may arise during and after the tea break advised for this activity? What strategy will I have for dealing with them?

● Do I see a real need for this activity – can I justify running it – or are there other strategies available to me?

In its place, and with the 'right' group, this activity will work powerfully and promote positive group development, through acknowledgement of strong points and a frank exposure of problem areas which can be openly dealt with. It assumes an ability and maturity on the part of participants that they can sort out problems between themselves (after the training event) or, failing that, that you will be available to intervene or to be accessible for problem resolution.

The event is often a catalyst, and what it exposes often creates an ongoing need for problem-solving. Handled properly it can be a major force for positive team development and reduction of factional / intra-team competition and point-scoring – a common failing which diverts energy away from the central task in hand.

If you have any serious doubts about it, don't use it!

3 Teamwork

Activity 10
DEFINITE MAYBE

Description

Not so much an activity, more an introduction to decision-making. It initally asks participants to assess how decisive they are. The first exercise could stand alone, but leads naturally to a discussion of the decision-making processes, and the problems of having to make quick but sound decisions at a time of rapid growth and change. Steps towards effective decision-making are discussed in small group and plenary sessions.

Aim

To enable participants to understand and be able to apply effective decision-making processes.

Time

2 hours; could be run across more than one session

Resources

- Copy of Exercise – Sheet A for each participant
- Copy of Exercise – Sheet B for each participant
- Copy of Exercise – Sheet C for each participant
- Copy of Handout for each participant
- Pen/pencil for each participant
- Clipboard, or table/desk space for each participant
- Flipchart and marker pen for trainer use

Method

1 Trainer input: to explain that the activity comprises several stages. It begins with each participant taking a critical look at their own decisiveness, and progresses to suggest ways in which the decision-making process can be made more objective, i.e. by following certain steps of deduction, and/or by involving others as appropriate.

2 Issue Exercise – Sheet A, which is a self–report questionnaire. This is not an in-depth psychological study of levels of decisiveness, but a fairly light-hearted introduction to the subject. It may be best to suggest that participants stick to decision-making at work in answering the questions.

3 Inform participants that they have five minutes to complete the questionnaire. Explain that individuals need not ponder over each question; their immediate 'gut reaction' is what is called for.

4 Explain the marking procedure, as shown on Exercise – Sheet B. It would be helpful to write this on a flipchart or reproduce copies to issue as a handout to accompany the questionnaire. These profiles are merely an indication of decisiveness; levels of decisiveness depend on a variety of factors and circumstances. It should also be remembered that indecisiveness, in one context, is not such a bad thing. After all, a quick decision is not always a good decision!

5 Allow participants to comment on the questionnaire. Ask whether participants considered the profiles a relatively accurate description of their attitude to decision-making.

Steps 1–5 can stand alone as an introduction to problem-solving and decision-making. Continue from Step 6 if you wish this to be a complete introduction to training in the decision-making process.

6 Trainer input on decision making. Several points need to be made about the quality of decision-making. Everyone is constantly making decisions, whether about crucial issues or deciding whether to wait for another 15 minutes before taking a coffee break. The quality of life, your success or failure, your high self-regard or low self-esteem, are the sum of the hundreds of decisions, large and small, made every day. These decisions are governed by past experience, 'What happened last time I did . . .?', on personal belief systems 'If I do . . . then . . . will happen', on how our decisions might affect other people, 'If I decide to do . . . he will think . . . of me' and so on.

Work decisions, which affect the organisation, the section, or your colleagues, need to be considered rationally. Although one viable decision is to decide to maintain the *status quo*, most decisions involve change, and the impact of this change upon individuals, the section, or organisation, needs to be carefully considered.

A way to avoid indecisiveness, and of looking at the decision-making process as objectively as possible, is to analyse what is involved, and pursue the various stages in a systematic way.

7 Identify the stages required in decision-making. This can either be done by discussion with the group, flipcharting the stages as they are identified, or by issuing and talking through the Handout.

8 If you have not done so at Step 7, issue the Handout.

9 Using a flipchart, list as many kinds of viable decisions as participants can think of. These can include:

- a top management decision – imposed and needing to be implemented
- a consensus decision, made by a team
- an expert decision, made by one person designated to decide for the group
- a majority decision; some may still disagree
- a 'yes' decision; a positive green light for action
- a 'no' decision; the thumbs down, a positive rejection
- the decision to make no decision at present; taken consciously, with forethought and careful consideration, this is a valid and responsible option
- difficult decisions – someone once said 'difficult decisions are more difficult to make in difficult times' and this is certainly true of the present world of tight economies and rapid change – there is less margin for error
- obscure decisions – what is required is already known; how to put it into practice is the issue
- weak decisions; the easy way out, often opted for but seldom effective
- shared decisions – share the risk, the glory or the blame
- political decisions – political with a small 'p', aimed to placate certain people. A decision is seen to be made, but leads to nothing.

These are a few of the sorts of decisions which might be made. There are also 'good' decisions, but one can only know they are good with hindsight

– everyone is fallible. There are 'bad' decisions, and the same is true. What must be done is to explore all options before deciding. There will be no guarantees that the correct decision has been reached, but at least everything possible will have been done to get it right.

10 Consider the quality and acceptance factors in decision making. The quality of a decision depends on its ultimate size and impact. For example, a high-quality decision might involve the consideration of complex data, or the saving or expenditure of large sums of money. The acceptance of a decision is the extent to which it affects the workforce – 'What's in it for me?' or, more commonly, 'How will it affect my hours, system of work, pay, future?' and so on.

Using the above analysis, there are four areas of decision making:

- high acceptance, low quality – matter a great deal to employees, but have no major effect on the organisation in terms of finance and so on

- high acceptance, high quality – have important financial implications and also affect employees greatly

- low acceptance, low quality – small matters neither affecting management nor workforce greatly

- low acceptance, high quality – decisions which have high technical or financial importance, but which do not directly affect the workforce

11 Issue Exercise – Sheet C which shows diagrammatically the above analysis and poses some questions for participants.

12 Divide participants into syndicate groups. Instruct them to discuss the questions and be ready to present their conclusions to the whole group in 20–30 minutes. Give a time check after 20 minutes; renegotiate times if necessary.

Discussions will inevitably prove that there are grey areas, but at least participants will begin to have a feel for the types of approach which may ease possible friction when introducing change, and to be more decisive when faced with having ultimate responsibility for the decision-making process.

13 After the allocated time, reassemble the group and ask for comments on the syndicate group discussions. Go through each question asking groups' assessment of the situation, what type of issue it is (e.g. low quality, low acceptance) and how they would go about the decision-making process. The final answers to this will depend on the context and on the values of the organisation and possibly other factors, so 'correct answers'

are not provided. What *is* important here is that there is a consensus resulting from discussion of the issues involved.

Questions you might use:

- Who is affected by the decision?
- Who should be consulted?
- What sort of information is necessary to reach an informed decision?
- What are the alternatives to maintaining the *status quo* if the suggested proposal is not accepted?
- What methods should be used to resolve issues where two sides' interests are basically incompatible?
- What sorts of issues should be left for top management decision?
- What sorts of issues should involve employees?

14 Process the entire activity.

Questions you might use:

- Although this should only be seen as an introduction, in what ways has this helped your understanding of decision-making?
- How does careful consideration of options, consultation and so on help the decision-making process?
- In which areas are your hands tied regarding decision-making at work?
- In what ways can you now be more decisive in the workplace?

15 Close the activity.

EXERCISE – SHEET A:
HOW DECISIVE ARE YOU?

	Often	Sometimes	Rarely	Never
1 Do you put off making important decisions?	☐	☐	☐	☐
2 Do you lie awake at night agonising over difficult decisions?	☐	☐	☐	☐
3 After making decisions, do you then have second thoughts?	☐	☐	☐	☐
4 Do you go back on decisions?	☐	☐	☐	☐
5 Do other people's opinions affect your decisions?	☐	☐	☐	☐
6 Do you feel you need to iron out every little detail before arriving at a decision?	☐	☐	☐	☐
7 Would you rather someone else made decisions on your behalf?	☐	☐	☐	☐
8 Do you make a decision, and then spend hours regurgitating the facts, hoping you've made the right decision?	☐	☐	☐	☐
9 Have you missed opportunities because you've procrastinated for too long?	☐	☐	☐	☐
10 Do you do any task however unimportant and trivial rather than face up to making a difficult decision?	☐	☐	☐	☐

	Often	Sometimes	Rarely	Never
11 Have you gone to your boss for a decision which you should have been qualified to make alone?	☐	☐	☐	☐
12 Did you hesitate as you answered these questions?	☐	☐	☐	☐

EXERCISE – SHEET B:
SCORING YOUR QUESTIONNAIRE

Give yourself two points for every 'often' ticked; three points for every 'sometimes'; four points for every 'rarely' and five points for each 'never'.

If you scored between the maximum, 60, and 50 points you could be said to be decisive. You are quite prepared to take responsibility for your choices. However, sometimes it pays to weigh up all the pros and cons before making decisions, and a little concern over the finer points can often lead to better decision-making.

If you scored between 50 and 35 you may have to be a bit more consistent in your decision-making. Some decisions are not easy for you, but ultimately you have the responsibility to make choices and keep to them. You need to find a balance between gathering all the facts possible within a reasonable time period, then making an informed decision without going over and over the facts, or holding a post-mortem after the event.

If your score was below 35 the chances are that you are, at this moment, procrastinating over decision-making either in your work or home life. You need to be more decisive. You are the one who is going to be the most stressed if you don't. Self-confidence can be gained by studying methods and stages of problem-solving and decision-making, and applying these theories until decisiveness becomes second nature to you.

HANDOUT – STAGES REQUIRED IN DECISION-MAKING

Decision-making should entail four distinct phases:

1 *Define the problem*. While not suggesting that all decisions stem from problems *per se*, you must define exactly what is to be dealt with before a decision can be reached. Quite often, what is seen are symptoms rather than the crux of the issue itself. What seem to be key elements are often merely the most visible ones. It may be helpful to break down issues on which decisions have to be reached, into component parts.

2 *Analyse the problem*. Assemble all the relevant data. Ask yourself who is to make the ultimate decision? Who must be consulted? Who must be informed? What will be the impact of the decision on other areas and functions? and so on. By spending time on this stage it becomes clear whether or not the situation has, in fact, been clearly defined.

3 *Consider all possible solutions*. Having defined and analysed the situation, it is important to develop all possible solutions. Either / or options are not enough. Use logical thinking to evaluate data; lateral thinking to turn the problem on its head and inside out to ensure that the issue has been looked at from every conceivable angle. The pros and cons of each option should be considered before deciding on what should be the appropriate course of action. In most decisions, because of this methodical sifting, the final range of feasible choices will be far smaller than the original list of options.

4 *Decide on the best solution*. In deciding on the best solution, five criteria need to be considered:

● the risk involved – should the present be sacrificed for future gain, for example?

● economy of effort – which option gives the greatest result from the least effort?

● time-scale – long- and short-term aspects; is achieving the first step sufficient in the short term, or must there be instant results?

● resources available – do we have the financial, material and human resources to carry this through?

● people – are those affected by the decision likely to be committed to it? Do they have the skills, competence and understanding to carry it out? Would we need to train existing staff or recruit new people?

Finally, having made the decision it must be followed through to the point of action. One of the most difficult aspects of decision-making is ensuring that those whom your decision affects understand, are committed to and take ownership of the action needed to put the decision into practice.

Activity 11

DYNAMICS

Description

This is a multifaceted activity involving teamwork. It includes a practical assignment (setting objectives, problem-solving, creative thinking, planning and production of an end product), and looks at the processes involved in executing the assignment (communication, leadership, allocation of tasks, participation and so on).

Aim

To develop team effectiveness through an understanding of the concepts of content and process.

Time

2 hours

Resources

• Sheets of flipchart paper and markers.

• Construction materials: sheets of A3 and A4 paper, pencils, scissors, ruler, paper fasteners, paper clips, adhesive tape, string, rubber bands, stapler, buttons, needle and thread etc.

NB Not all of the above need be supplied, but sufficient materials are needed for group(s) to construct a paper model with moving parts.

• (Optional) Copy of Trainer notes as a handout for each participant.

Method

1 Trainer input: to explain that the activity is in two parts. Explain the purpose, procedure and timings for the first part of the exercise. The task for the group(s) is to construct a three-dimensional paper elephant, with moving parts, using the materials provided. Groups should work on the premiss that the finished elephant is to be a prototype for a paper-craft kit for children, and should be presented, at the end of the given time, complete with instructions on how to make it.

2 If necessary, divide the group into smaller syndicate groups. The activity is more fun if competitive (if appropriate, a small prize can be awarded for the best prototype). However, it is important to keep work teams together.

3 Make available materials from which the paper elephant will be constructed. Issue sheets of flipchart paper and markers on which should be written the list of assembly instructions.

4 Instruct the team(s) that 45 minutes will be allowed to design and construct the prototype and to compile the assembly instructions. Remind the team(s) of the 'rules': paper elephant; three dimensional; moving parts; for construction by children; appropriate list of instructions.

5 Observe the group(s) closely. Who takes the role of leader? Who initiates ideas? Who supports ideas? Who clarifies ideas? Who writes the list of instructions? Who talks most? Who listens well? Who influences decisions? How are conflicts resolved? etc.

6 At the end of the given time, instruct the team(s) to present their prototype and to go through the assembly instructions, explaining the thought processes behind the construction.

7 Assess the prototype(s). If participants have been working in small groups, judge the models – trainer's decision final! Allow a short time for participants to 'unpack' their thoughts about the task of designing and building a paper elephant.

Questions you might use:

- How easy was the task? Why was it easy (or why wasn't it)?
- Did you feel you worked well as a team?
- How did you decide on the final design?
- How were the *principles* involved in accomplishing this task – setting objectives for action, using a problem-solving approach, giving and gathering opinions, analysing suggestions and so on – similar to the way your team operates in the workplace? In what way did they differ?

8 Thank the group(s) for participating in the task and explain that the design and construction of the prototype paper elephant was the first part of an activity about 'content' and 'process'. Explain the difference to the group (*see* Trainer notes). Part one – the task itself – was about content. The rest of the activity looks at the process involved – how the team(s) organised themselves, how decisions were made, what happened in the group(s) – group dynamics.

9 Lead a discussion on how the group(s) functioned as a team. (Some of the 'process' discussion may have been started at Step 7 above).

Questions you might use:

- How were team roles determined?
- Who took the lead?
- (To this person) Did you realise that you had adopted this role/are you usually team leader? Is this a role you usually adopt in teams – work and social?
- Is it appropriate for the same person always to lead, whatever the task? Why, or why not?
- Who spoke the most? Were your ideas adopted . . . adapted . . . rejected?
- When individuals' ideas were rejected how did they feel?
- As a team, how do you think you handled feelings?
- Who questioned ideas that were put forward . . . asked for clarification?
- Who supported . . . encouraged . . . helped other team members?
- Were there differences of opinion? How were these resolved?
- Is it a good or bad thing to air differences of opinion?
- How did you decide on the final design?
- Was there consensus, compromise, or did one person decide?
- Did anyone contribute more than others?
- Did anyone not contribute?
- In the workplace, why is it important to identify reasons for high or low participation in team tasks?
- Whose responsibility is it to ensure that all team members contribute?
- Why is it important for all team members to contribute?

10 Ensure that every participant's contribution to their team has been acknowledged and discussed. For example, you could briefly discuss the importance of the 'scribe'/notetaker – does he or she just record group decisions or is there an editing role through seeking clarification and interpreting meaning.

11 Explain that *how* a team achieves its purpose and accomplishes a task – the process – is crucial to the quality of the end product (*see* Trainer notes). The output achieved in terms of team tasks will be of poor quality if poor quality processes are adopted.

Effective teams are those in which every member has a part to play. The exercise will have shown natural abilities of individuals as team members and in some cases the need for adaptability to meet the needs of a particular task. Roles will vary within teams depending on the nature of the work in hand, and individuals should recognise their own strengths and consolidate them, learn to be flexible within teams to meet the common good, and acknowledge weaknesses and work towards improvement in these areas.

12 (Optional) Issue the Trainer notes as a handout.

13 Close the activity.

TRAINER NOTES

Content and process

Content is the 'what': possibly the aim or overall task of a team; it is the word used to describe the substance of the task itself. If a team has decided to work on solving a complex problem, then the problem itself is the content.

Process is the 'how': how the team achieves its purpose and accomplishes its task. It is about the ways in which the individual members work together and interact with one another in carrying out tasks, regardless of the task itself. In the problem–solving example the process would be the application of various techniques such as creative thinking, communication, sharing ideas, analysis, how the group motivates itself and so on.

High quality processes recognise the needs of individual members, and the team as an entity in itself.

There are several aspects to the process which need to be addressed if teams are to function effectively. A leadership style which is democratic and which allows leadership to be shared tends to produce higher quality group processes.

Members should practise open and honest communication. A significant factor is the level and quality of listening within the team. 'Splinter group' discussions should be avoided when one member is addressing the team; everyone should be encouraged to contribute; minority views should be treated positively; members should be encouraged to express openly ideas, opinions, priorities, disagreements and feelings. Conflict should be seen as a positive force; *productive* conflict resolution is the ideal.

Every member should participate fully and teams need to be aware of, and identify reasons for, low levels of participation. This needs to be addressed if the team is to function to full capacity.

Too often individuals and teams concentrate almost exclusively on the content aspect of their work, and therefore most teams, most of the time, do not achieve the quality of output (content) of which they are capable. An effective team is one which addresses equally content and process issues.

Activity 12

• •

ARE YOU WITH US?

Description

A light–hearted activity to help identify individuals who are working effectively as team members and to test teamwork in action.

Aim

To assess team skills, especially problem-solving and creative/lateral thinking. It should also indicate which members of a group are team oriented, who has leadership skills, who are more naturally 'followers', who promote and who obstruct teamwork, and so on.

Time

30 minutes

Resources

- One sheet of A4 paper per team
- (Available in the course room) More sheets of A4; scissors, adhesive tape, paper clips, pencils, stapler etc.

Method

Have available in the course room, but do not draw attention to, sheets of A4 paper for practice purposes, and the means to cut, stick or staple pieces of paper together.

1 Explain that the activity is about teamwork.

2 Place a sheet of A4 paper, per work team represented, on a clear space of floor in the course room, and allocate one piece of paper to each team.

3 Ask all participants *who feel part of their team* to go and stand on their sheet of A4 paper. (Observe which individuals, if any, show reluctance to go to the paper or, indeed, refuse to go at all. This *could* indicate that they do not feel part of the team; this should be followed up later. Do not indulge in recriminations, bullying or cajoling at this stage.)

4 Issue the following instructions depending on the number of people in each team. Use these exact words:

Three or four people 'the heels and toes of both feet must be on the paper' *Five to eight people* 'both feet must be on the paper' *More than eight people* 'at least one foot must be on the paper'.

5 It should become immediately obvious, that without physical contortions, it is impossible to fulfil the task without adjusting the proportions of the sheets of A4 paper (*see* Trainer notes 1 on how this might be achieved). Observe who takes the lead; who offers suggestions on how the task might be accomplished; who (if any) suggests they use other materials available in the course room; who prefers to analyse all possibilities before proceeding to act; who prefer to 'follow' or take on the part of workers; who is supportive; who is obstructive, and so on.

6 When all teams have achieved the task (or when it is obvious that some might never) assess the attempts. To keep the light-heartedness of the activity alive, you could give a small prize to the most enterprising and successful team – fun-size chocolate bars or something similar.

7 Ask participants to return to the main group. Tease out the learning points of the activity through group discussion.

Questions you might use:

- Did you enjoy the activity? What did you like about it? What did you dislike about it? What did you learn about your colleagues during the activity? (These questions are intended to help participants 'unpack' the experience of the activity itself, and should be kept light.)

- How did you go about solving the problem? Who led? Is this because you are usually seen as team leader? If not, what is unusual about this situation? Who suggested possible solutions? Who analysed the situation before acting. Did you make use of equipment, such as scissors, available in the course room? Why (or why not?) Do you now feel that you all used your initiative to the full? Can you now see alternative/ better solutions?

- Why were some of you reluctant (or refused) to participate? Do you all see yourselves as part of your team(s)? What does being part of a team involve? Does it include pulling together – even in situations like the one just experienced? What is the difference between being part of a group and being part of a team? (*see* Trainer notes 2) How do feel you responded to this activity – as a group, or as a team?

- What have you learned from this activity? How can you apply this learning back in the workplace? What needs to be done to make your teamwork more effective?

8 Close the activity by thanking the group for participating, and for being good sports!

Variation

If more than one team is involved, the activity could be made competitive from the start. Issue materials such as scissors and adhesive to each team. Set a time limit, and state that the most enterprising means of solving the problem will 'win'. The best design will be judged on evidence of teamwork, and the ingenuity of the solution. Trainer's decision is final!

Judging should be based on three things:

1 observation: how well each member was committed to the common goal; the level of mutual support; the amount of shared communication and so on

2 on the final result e.g. when standing on the transformed sheet of A4, are the participants in a line (more like the bus queue) or 'together' (more like a rugby scrum)

3 the success of the design.

TRAINER NOTES 1

The following are just three ways in which one sheet of A4 might be used to meet the criteria of the activity

1

a) Fold sheet lengthways to define halfway mark; fold outside edges into centre.

b) Again, fold outside into centre.

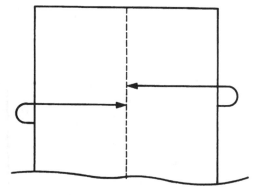

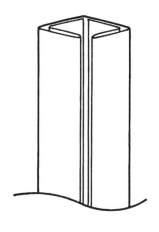

c) Fold all in half along centre line. You should now have a folded strip approximately 1" wide.

d) Make cuts with scissors as shown almost to the edges of the strip.

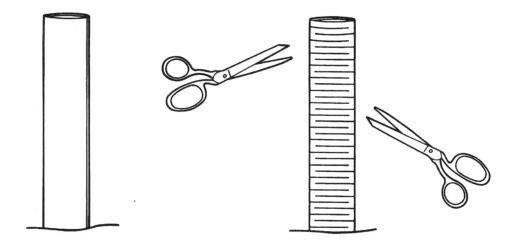

e) Open out carefully. By pulling the short edges, the sheet of A4 should now measure up to three times its original length.

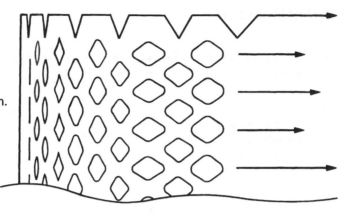

2   Cut the paper as indicated on the diagram. The 'spiral' ends can be joined to form one long loop on which all team members can stand.

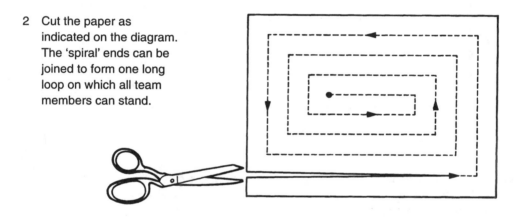

3   Simply cut the paper into strips and reassemble. (If teams make one long strip and stand along it, does the resulting 'line' of people represent teamwork as much as if, say, the strips were reassembled to form a square or rectangle?)

TRAINER NOTES 2

Ask the group to define the difference between a group of people and a team. The following notes may help lead discussion.

Generally speaking, a group can be any collection of individuals. A bus queue comprises a group of people, with very little in common besides the shared need to catch a bus – not even necessarily the same bus. They will not all have the same destination, and therefore very little by way of a common cause. In the work situation, groups may very well be collections of individuals, most working independently – sometimes even at cross-purposes with others.

Teams, however, are groups of individuals with a common purpose and set of objectives. Team members are interdependent, and use mutual support to achieve team goals. Continuing the 'goal' analogy, footballers, operating independently, would achieve very little without the collective effort of all – i.e. teamwork.

In the context of this activity, participants have to accept and identify with the common objective, otherwise they will not perceive themselves to be a team.

Activity 13
• •
INTERLUDES

Description

Exercises to stimulate creativity and explore both logical and lateral thinking in problem-solving. It is suggested that they be used as 'fun' problems for participants to solve during breaks, or perhaps as warm–ups each morning or even overnight as 'homework' rather than as training sessions *per se*.

Aim

To stimulate mental agility and problem-solving skills

Time

Flexible

Resources

- Paper and pencil/pen for each participant
- Copies of the Exercises specified in the Trainer notes
- Flipchart and marker pen for trainer use

Method

(*Before participants arrive*)

1 Prepare flipchart sheets with copies of the exercises (*see* Trainer notes).

2 Ensure that there is sufficient paper and pens/pencils in the course room for participant use.

(*At beginning of activity*)

3 Explain the purpose of the exercises. These exercises are designed to be challenging but fun. Individually, in similar form, they have been included in several publications, so some may be known to some participants. If this is the case, those 'in the know' are asked to keep the solutions from their colleagues.

There will be a different exercise on the flipchart each (day/morning/ break and so on). There will be no Brownie points for correct answers; just the satisfaction of solving the problem as set.

The reason for including these free-time activities during the training course is to give participants the opportunity to test their mental agility and powers of both logical and lateral thinking. (Some exercises require the former; others the latter). This is good preparation for contributing to a participative training course, and sound practice for anyone who has to survive in a world of constant and rapid change.

4 At a suitable point in the course run the exercises. Six exercises have been included; there are many others of a similar kind which would be suitable. The activity is presented as a concept, i.e. to give participants something relevant and challenging to do over coffee, or before the course begins each morning. Don't labour the processing of these exercises, although it is important to set them in the general context so participants can see the point of doing them.

TRAINER NOTES

Exercise 1

Instructions

Connect all nine crosses using just four straight lines. At no time should your pen leave the paper. There can be no retracing, although lines may cross if necessary.

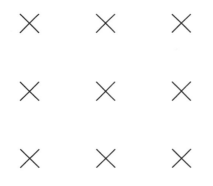

A solution:

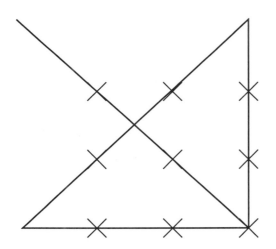

This is just one solution; there are others, equally valid. Ask participants who found the task difficult why this was. Usually it is because of the rigidity and inflexibility of our perceptions. We see the imaginary boundary – in this case a square – presented, and do not consider going beyond boundaries, either real or imagined. Thus rules and regulations inhibit our creativity in devising solutions to problems.

For those who found the task easy, or had prior experience of the exercise, now try joining the crosses with just three straight lines. The concept is the same as the solution offered above, i.e. removing from the mind the obvious boundary of the square shape suggested by the positioning of the crosses on the page. Nowhere does it say that the lines must go *through* the centre of the crosses. Provided the crosses are connected, and therefore touched by one of three straight lines, the solution criteria are met.

Solution:

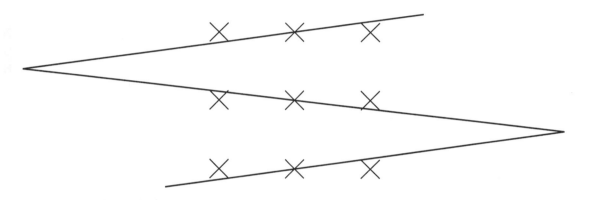

Exercise 2

This is just a simple anagram, and should present no problems for anyone used to crossword puzzles and word quizzes. However, it is surprising how few discover the solution.

Instructions:

Make one word, in everyday usage, from the letters shown below

ROAST MULES

Solution:

SOMERSAULT

The reason why most people find difficulty in solving this anagram is that although the word is known to virtually everyone who has English as a first language, it is a word seldom written down, and thus seldom read. It is therefore unfamiliar to us. In problem-solving, we tend to always look for the familiar.

Ask those who solved the anagram what methods they used.

Exercise 3

Instructions:

Count the number of triangles presented in this diagram. (It would be useful for participants to duplicate the diagram on their own paper, and use some method of over-lining to identify individual triangles).

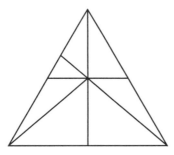

In fact there are over 20 different triangles. Establish how many triangles participants identified, and who identified the most. Ask this person to demonstrate how they arrived at their particular total. Ask if anyone else saw other triangles not identified by this demonstration.

This exercise can raise the issues of individual versus collaborative problem-solving. It could also be used to introduce a session on conflict – often the result of individuals' different perceptions, or distortion of reality.

Exercise 4

It is important that you draw the books as shown below so that participants have something visual and tangible to work from.

Instructions:

There are four hardback books on a shelf, volumes of poetry, all exactly the same size with the same number of pages. They are arranged in order, volumes 1, 2, 3 and 4. The covers and spines are made of card one sixth of an inch thick; collectively, the pages of each volume are exactly two inches thick.

If a bookworm started eating its way through the volumes at page 1 of volume 1, and ate through to the last page of volume 4, how far had it travelled?

Solution: 5 inches.

Answers usually range from 7–9$\frac{1}{3}$ inches. Very few people get the correct answer first time. Sometimes it helps to do the calculations without the use of the visual aid. Think of a book on a shelf. The first page of a volume will be on the right, the last page on the left of the books as seen on the shelf. Therefore, calculations should begin with the second cover of volume 1 and continue through to the left-hand cover (as seen) on volume 4 – a total of six individual covers plus two sets of pages i.e. $(6 \times \frac{1}{6}) = 1 + (2 \times 2) = 4$ gives a total of 5.

Often it is the most familiar situation which causes us the greatest difficulty when trying to look at things differently or creatively. We are so used to handling books with the first page next to the left-hand cover and the last page nearest the right, that it is difficult to solve this puzzle where books are seen in a somewhat less familiar position, from a different perspective, and the order of pages therefore reversed.

Exercise 5

This exercise requires participants to look for alternative meanings to well known words to find the common link

Instructions:

Insert the words missing from the brackets

Example: crow (......) swindle
            crow (rook) swindle

1 dance (......) sphere

2 shore (......) land

3 sheep (......) collar

4 enclosure (......) crush

5 staff (......) criminal

Solutions:

1 BALL

2 BEACH

3 DOG

4 POUND

5 CROOK

Exercise 6

Instructions:

What are the missing numbers in the following sequences

1   4   9   20   43   __

2

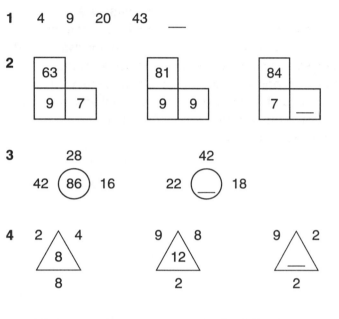

3   28   42

   42 (86) 16   22 (__) 18

4   2 ⋀ 4   9 ⋀ 8   9 ⋀ 2

   8   12   __

   8   2   2

5   Which number comes next in the following
    sequence, 3, 12, or 20?

   8   11   15   14   19   1   7   __

Solutions

1 90
   Each number is twice the preceding one, plus one, two, three, and finally four
   (43 × 2 = 86 + 4 = 90).
2 12
   The number in the top box is the result of multiplying the numbers in the
   bottom two boxes.
3 82
   Halve each of the numbers outside the circle; add the resulting three numbers and multiply by two (21 + 11 + 9 = 41 × 2 = 82).
4 6
   Multiply the three numbers outside the triangle. The number inside each triangle is the square root of this total (9 × 2 = 18 × 2 = 36. 6 × 6 = 36).

5 3

The sequence depends not on logical mathematical reasoning, but on the way the words are spelt. Thus eleven comes before fifteen, and fifteen comes before fourteen alphabetically, and so on. From the given options, three comes before both twelve and twenty in alphabetical order.

Most participants will find questions 1–4 relatively easy because there is a logical solution; given enough time they can be worked out by anyone who is numerate. Question 5 usually poses more difficulty – especially following, as it does, a series of logical exercises – because it requires lateral thinking, translating the numbers into words and arranging them alphabetically. This is another example of the importance of being able to look at problems from different perspectives – discarding the familiar, turning the situation upside down and inside out to pursue every possible approach.

Activity 14

••

LADDER OR TABLES?

Description

A simple activity to free the mind from logical thinking and to encourage creative thought. Relevant to a wide range of training issues to do with quality or customer care; for example change, problem-solving, human resource management or team building.

Aim

To encourage a creative, team-orientated approach to problem-solving and to enable participants to identify the benefits of this.

Time

45 minutes – 1 hour

Resources

- Space for syndicate groups to work in isolation and for plenary session
- Table space or a clipboard on which to rest papers for each participant
- Flipchart and marker pen for trainer use
- Copy of the Exercise for each participant
- Paper, pen/pencil for each participant
- Copy of Trainer notes
- (Optional) Small prize for winning team, e.g. chocolate bar, bag of sweets

Method

1 Trainer input: to introduce the activity. Quite often, when confronted with an abstract visual image, our eyes and brains 'see' something which is unique to us – the person standing next to us may 'see' something entirely different – but once that message has got through to the brain it is very difficult to perceive anything else in that image. This has been shown through psychological tests such as the famous ink-blot test. I might see a tiger in the jungle; you may see a dog curled up in front of the fire, hidden in the same ink blot. However, once that perception is fixed, it's hard to see anything else – unless it's pointed out and explained. Then we may

accept an alternative interpretation.

The same principle applies to problem-solving. As soon as one solution presents itself, we tend to become blinkered. It is difficult to shift viewpoints; to look at the situation from another, entirely different angle.

This simple activity is intended to help unlock the mind from vertical thinking; to show that there are several ways of defining a situation, problem, or, in this case, an image. It will also illustrate the value of sharing ideas – another concept important to problem-solving.

It is a useful exercise in the context of new product ideas, improved office systems, different marketing angles and so on. All these benefit from **everyone** in the organisation – at **all** levels – improving their creative thinking ability and working as a cohesive team. This activity also addresses these issues.

2 Explain procedure and timings. The group will be divided into syndicate groups. (Syndicate group size will depend on the total number of participants as the activity benefits from having two or more syndicate groups in competitive mode.)

Each individual will be given a sheet of paper and pencil/pen and a copy of the exercise which has a shape printed on it. Participants will work individually, at first, to see how many different descriptions of the shape they can think of. They will then be asked to share their thoughts with other members of their syndicate group, and draw up a collective list, adding to the descriptions as they think of them. The syndicate group with the most descriptions 'wins'.

3 Divide the group into syndicate groups. If possible, arrange it so that syndicate groups can work without being overlooked or overheard.

4 Issue paper, a pen or pencil, and a copy of the exercise to each participant. Remind them that until you tell them to stop, participants should work independently, without conferring with their colleagues, to devise as many different descriptions of the shape as possible.

5 Allow about five minutes for participants to work alone, then instruct participants to share their ideas with other members of their syndicate group. They have another 15 minutes to write up a collective list.

6 Ask syndicate groups how many different descriptions they have managed to produce. Announce the 'winning' team and award any optional prize.

7 Write up the group's collective list on flipchart paper. In fairness to each syndicate group, take one description from each team in rotation until all

syndicate group lists have been exhausted. Allow syndicate representatives to illustrate their perceptions where required.

8 Add any observations/ideas from the Trainer notes not already included.

9 First, process the participants' experience of the activity itself, then draw out the learning points, relating them to the work situation.

Questions you might use:

- Working independently, how did you get on?
- Did anyone find it easy to come up with several descriptions?
- Did anyone get stuck on just one or two?
- How did team efforts compare with individual 'scores'?
- What lessons can be drawn from this? (e.g. *individuality* v. *group work* v. *teamwork)*
- Did any syndicate group list as many descriptions as the final tally from the whole group?
- If so, were there still new descriptions which other syndicate groups had devised but which did not feature on your lists?
- What lessons can be drawn from this? (e.g. *interdepartmental co-operation)*
- Were you surprised at the number/variety of descriptions of this simple shape?
- Did you 'turn' or 'dissect' the image in order to arrive at a new perspective on it? Why could this be useful (e.g. *lateral thinking in problem-solving)*
- How can the lessons learned from this simple activity be applied in the workplace?
- What benefits can you think of in approaching a task or problem with both logical and creative thinking?

10 Close the activity.

 **EXERCISE**

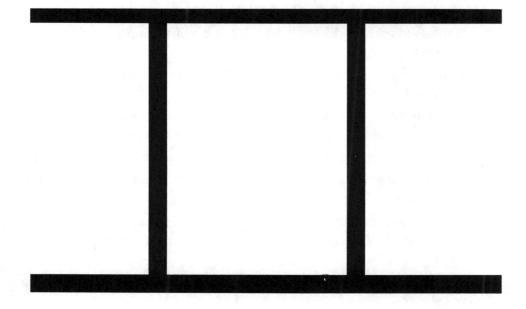

TRAINER NOTES

The following may offer some guidance regarding the possible interpretations of the figure drawn in the exercise:

1 The Roman numeral 2
2 Pi (Π)
3 Part of a ladder
4 Two tables, one upturned, standing on each other
5 Small section of a guitar fretboard and strings
6 Prisoner and visitor holding hands across table
7 Four capital letter T's joined up

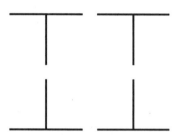

8 Four pairs of capital L's back to back and joined up

9 Cross-section of a cardboard box with its flaps up
10 Fencing
11 Jump, at a dog agility trial
12 Clothes drier
13 Indoor aerial
14 Two capital I's (serif)
15 Jail bars
16 Banner on two poles
17 Capped chimney
18 Leg, between bottom of shorts and top of wellingtons
19 Two capital H's end to end

20 Dynamiting plunger
21 Bottle neck and stopper
22 'Proud' nail
23 Window
    (and here you've *really* got to use your imagination!)
24 Legs of matchstick woman (standing in water?)

25 Head of a 'Scottie' dog

Activity 15

COMMITMENT

Description

An activity whereby participants are asked to see proposed changes from the perspectives of both management and workforce. The trainer/manager should also get an insight into what steps should be taken to maximise commitment to a new project or venture.

Aim

To make participants aware of the issues needed to be addressed by management in order to effect change and gain commitment from those affected by it.

Time

45 minutes – 1 hour

Resources

- Copy of Exercise – 'Commitment' for each participant
- Pens/pencils

Method

1 If necessary, divide participants into syndicate groups. It would help if groups comprise people with similar roles/from within similar organisations.

2 Issue exercise sheets to each participant. Instruct groups that they should choose one topic to discuss – one which has the most relevance to their own work situation, or which they could foresee as having a possible relevance for the future. They should consider:

- the sort of procedure usually followed by management when introducing change within their organisations
- the areas where insufficient information is presently given
- the sorts of issues which *should* be addressed by management in order to gain commitment to change
- the exact procedure they would follow to gain commitment to the topic chosen from the Exercise sheet.

3 Allow 15–30 minutes for syndicate group deliberation. Circulate to give advice on procedure, to prompt if necessary to get discussion going, and to ensure that the talk is not getting too anecdotal!

4 Reassemble main group and receive feedback. First, allow the group(s) to talk about their reaction to the exercise itself, again keeping anecdotes to the minimum.

Questions you might use:

- Were any of the scenarios close to a situation you have experienced, or are likely to encounter?
- Is it difficult to become committed to change which involves more work or personal sacrifice?
- Can you see anything positive, for the workforce, in any of the scenarios presented? If yes, what exactly? (Organisational profitability/competitiveness giving greater job security; flexi-time allows for accumulation of time due – additional days off, hours to better fit travel/domestic arrangements; redistribution of duties gives variety, opportunity to learn new skills; more responsibility can give greater job satisfaction etc.)

Next, concentrate on the four questions posed, and work through these for each scenario discussed by the group(s).

Questions you might use:

- How are decisions made regarding issues such as the one you've been discussing? Who is involved? Who is consulted? At what stage are you involved?
- What background information are you given as to why a proposal has been made or decision reached?
- How, if at all, would it help if you were better informed?
- Generally, is commitment greater in individuals who are part of the planning and decision-making process?
- How might management better gain commitment to proposed changes?
- Looking specifically at the scenario you chose to discuss, what should management do to gain commitment to the proposal? What are the likely pitfalls? How could these be overcome?

Finally, establish what individuals gained from the exercise, and how they might utilise the learning at their own place of work.

Questions you might use:

- How (if at all) has the activity helped you better understand the elements involved in gaining commitment to proposed change?
- What could you do, in your own areas of work, to ensure that changes you propose are seen more as a challenge than a threat?

5 Close the activity.

EXERCISE – COMMITMENT

In your group, discuss:

1 the sort of procedure usually followed by management when introducing change within your organisation(s)

2 the areas where insufficient information is presently given

3 the sorts of issues which *should* be addressed by management in order to gain commitment to change

4 the exact procedure you would follow to gain commitment to a topic chosen from the scenarios below.

Choose just one of the scenarios to work on – the one most closely related to your own work situation or which you could foresee having relevance in the future:

- increasing output by 15 per cent
- promoting a new, additional product range
- boosting sales to meet a heavily increased target
- introducing flexi-time to cover longer opening hours
- getting agreement to a wage freeze to avoid job losses
- redistribution of workloads / responsibilities to cover posts lost through redundancies / natural wastage.

Activity 16

• •

OLD DOGS, NEW TRICKS

Description

This is an activity for anyone who is responsible for helping adults to acquire new learning: skills, knowledge, attitudes. All of these may need to be changed, modified or simply gained in order to respond to new organisational climates.

Participants who might benefit would include:

- functional trainers
- temporary trainers (as defined in the introduction to this book)
- line managers and supervisors with a clear training role
- line staff with on-the-job training and/or coaching responsibilities

In carrying out the activity participants will be made aware of some basic assumptions which underpin much modern theory of adult learning.

The activity is demanding, intellectually, and uses an analytical approach which some people may find too abstract. You should satisfy yourself in advance that your group can benefit from it.

The activity seeks to explode one of the basic myths which constrains many adults and which results in fear of change : that 'You can't teach an old dog new tricks'. This is a familiar lament when people are asked to make changes in their established patterns of work or in their fundamental approach to work. Included in Handout 2 for this activity are some suggestions for further reading if participants (or, indeed, you) wish to pursue the theory further.

Aim

To introduce four basic assumptions of adult learning theory and to enable participants to draw on these assumptions in order to create effective learning experiences for themselves or their own staff.

Time

1 hour

Resources

- Overhead projector and screen
- Pre-prepared OHP transparency as specified in Trainer notes 1
- Flipchart and marker pen for trainer use
- Copy of Handout 1 for each participant
- Copy of Handout 2 for each participant

Method

1 Trainer input: to introduce the activity. Ask the group a direct question: 'Can you teach an old dog new tricks?' In other words how effectively do adults learn? Particularly, perhaps, older adults? Allow five minutes for a brief discussion on this.

2 Trainer input: to explain that, whatever the views expressed, all the research evidence which exists tends to show that adults learn just as effectively as children, but the techniques needed for learning to be effective may be different. Pedagogy is child learning theory. The term 'andragogy' was coined in the 1970s to cover adult learning theory and, although there is much healthy debate about whether andragogy is really different from pedagogy, we shall not concern ourselves with that here. What we shall do is to draw on a number of key concepts from andragogy.

   So far as learning and older people are concerned evidence suggests that older people learn just as well as – and probably more thoroughly than – younger adults. However, they may take longer to learn, not because they are slowing up or losing grey cells but because they have a greater framework of experience against which to relate the new learning. They are probably less inclined to take things at face value than are their younger counterparts.

3 Trainer input: to introduce the four basic assumptions of adult learning. Use the OHP transparency and the background material provided in Trainer notes 1 and 2. Allow ten minutes for this, including questions. Participants will receive a Handout which summarises the points you are about to cover.

   We suggest you do not discuss these ideas in depth at this stage. The activity will allow for a fuller exploration, but do allow questions which seek to clarify understanding.

4 Ask the group to identify a need which is to involve them in managing the learning of others through the setting up of a learning event. It can be to do with skills, attitudes, knowledge or a combination of all three. This works

best if you can get the group to work with a real-life need which now faces them. You may get several issues identified, in which case you can assign a number of syndicate groups each to work on a different issue. If there is a major organisational change afoot, work with that, or some facet of it. Use the suggestions which follow only if all else fails.

- you need to set up a learning event for some staff in their forties who have, until now, been mainly 'backroom'. They are now going to be involved in meeting the public face to face and some of them have expressed concern about their interviewing skills.

- You are about to computerise the work of a section that has until now been reliant on manual, clerical systems. There is considerable evidence of staff concern at this, particularly among the older generation. The database software has been chosen and training machines are available in-house.

- In order to try to qualify for BS 5750 your company has established some rigorous new standards of customer care. There is evidence of some cynicism among existing staff about 'all this TQM stuff'.

5 Once you have agreed the case study/studies divide the group up into syndicate groups. Issue Handout 1. Ask them to consider the four basic assumptions of adult learning and to identify what the implications would be for the design of the learning event identified in Step 4. Ask each syndicate group to identify at least four such implications. Allow 20 minutes for this. Note that you are not asking the group to design the learning event itself, but rather to **identify the principles they would use in order to design an effective learning event**.

So, for example, is there any way in which the issue of self-direction could have a bearing on the design of a learning event? (*In the computer case, the ability for someone to work at their own pace and at times of their own choosing could be a significant concession to the self-direction need.*) This is quite a demanding exercise and you might wish to draw yourself on the contents of Handout 2 (not yet issued) for guidance as to the kinds of issues that participants should be looking for.

6 Reconvene the main group. Ask each syndicate group in turn to identify their implications and flipchart them as they emerge. Allow 15 minutes for this. Remind the group of the initial assumptions of adult learning. The main implications have been identified in the handout, but your group may identify others.

Questions you might use:

(These should be put in the sequential order in which they appear below as they relate to stages of the activity)

- Did people agree with the assumptions?
- Did the assumptions accord with people's own learning experiences?
- Which assumption does that implication spring from?
- What does that implication mean in practice?
- How could the actions suggested by that implication be achieved?
- What problems might there be in doing that?
- Can you give an example?

7 Close the activity by issuing Handout 2.

HANDOUT 1

Adult learning: four basic assumptions

1 Adults learn most effectively when they are self-directing.

2 Adults have a massive fund of experience, which they value, and around which they structure new learning.

3 Adults have a ready learning capacity which is unimpaired throughout life.

4 Adults learn most effectively when they can see immediate applications.

HANDOUT 2

Some implications of the four basic assumptions

- Adults need to be involved in analysing the learning need, in setting learning objectives and in sharing responsibility for learning and evaluation.
- Adults need a supportive learning climate.
- Adults learn from each other, not just from the 'teacher'; adults are a rich resource for learning.
- Evaluation of learning should be in terms of 'rediagnosis of need' rather than 'pass or fail'.
- New learning will be related to experience; adults may appear less open-minded than younger learners.
- Experiential learning techniques may work better in some situations than more formal, transmittal (or lecturing) techniques.
- Emphasising the application of learning in the 'real world' will be a major factor in the success of adult learning.
- A curriculum (or learning programme) would be problem-focused rather than subject-focused.
- The starting point for all adult learning would be the issues and concerns which adults bring with them.

(For further reading on adult learning *see* Bibliography, Brookfield; Knowles; Tight.)

TRAINER NOTES 1

Make OHP transparency as follows:

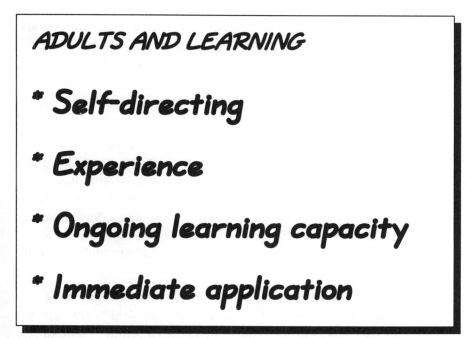

ADULTS AND LEARNING

* *Self-directing*

* *Experience*

* *Ongoing learning capacity*

* *Immediate application*

TRAINER NOTES 2

The four basic assumptions about adult learning, upon which most adult learning theory is based, are:

1 Adults learn most effectively when they are *self-directing*. In other words they are in control of their learning experience, set their own learning goals and manage the process of moving towards those goals in a way which they determine is best for them. They may choose what resources they want to draw on and they may choose what kind of learning method (or methods) they most favour.

2 Adults possess a substantial *fund of experience*, which they value, and around which they structure new learning. In other words, adults will be less inclined to take things at face value than children will. One extreme form would be the cynical comment 'I've seen it all before'. Adults who value their experience will not 'write it off' just to accommodate new ideas. New learning will be measured against experience and, if it conflicts, then both the new ideas and the experience may be called into question. 'Unlearning' is quite a difficult process for this reason.

3 Adults have a *ready learning capacity* which is unimpaired throughout life. In other words the 'old dog, new tricks' cliché has no validity. Adults are capable of learning at any age – which is not to say that all do, of course. However, many people would argue that life itself is a learning experience. (See also the comment in Step 2 about learning and older people.)

4 Adults learn most effectively when they can see *immediate applications* for the learning. In other words if the learning is clearly relevant and helpful to an adult's immediate need to do or change something the learning will be much more effective than, say, something abstract and not having any obvious immediate relevance. This is not to say that such things cannot be learned, of course. It's simply that the most effective learning takes place when immediate applications are clear.

These are assumptions and people may agree or disagree with them. However, they do form a basis for much adult learning theory and practice.

Activity 17

WINNING LEADERS

Description

An activity aimed specifically at those who are supervisors or team leaders, to raise awareness of the understanding, skills and qualities required for effective leadership.

Aim

To encourage greater awareness of leadership qualities and the need to review and, if necessary, modify approaches to leadership.

Time

2 hours – half a day. Much depends on the small-group discussion work, timings for which will depend on the individuals involved.

Resources

- Table top space, or clipboard on which participants can rest papers
- Pencil/pen for each participant
- Copy of Exercise for each participant
- Copy of Handout for each participant

Method

1 Trainer input: To explain leadership styles (*see* Trainer notes).

2 Trainer input: to explain procedure and timings. Initially participants will work independently completing a self-report questionnaire. This questionnaire is in three sections; each section contains 25 questions. Participants are required to answer 'yes', 'no', or if neither of these options is appropriate to write a few words in the 'other' box. The sections cover aspects essential to the leader's role, i.e. achieving the task, which is the reason why teams exist; developing and motivating individuals; maintaining effective relationships between the leader and the team and also between individuals within the team; sustaining morale and a sense of common purpose in meeting team and organisational objectives.

    Individuals will have 20 minutes to complete their personal questionnaires after which the main group will be divided into small syndicate groups where participant's reactions to the questionnaire can be discussed in small, supportive units. The timing for this second part of the activity can be negotiable, but should not exceed one hour.

3   Set up syndicate groups. If you get people into syndicate groups at this stage, they will be able to begin discussing the exercise as they finish, rather than wait for the slowest participant to complete the questionnaire.

4   Give one copy of the Exercise to each participant.

5   Begin the exercise. Remind participants that they have up to 20 minutes to complete the questionnaire.

6   When individuals have completed filling in the questionnaire, instruct them to look at each question and, within their syndicate group, discuss any issues arising.

   In most cases the appropriate response, if things are running efficiently and effectively, is obvious, e.g. 'Have you, and has each member of your team got a job specification?' should be answered by a 'Yes'. In syndicate group discussions, participants should pay particular attention to areas where it is clear work needs to be done to improve things, giving constructive suggestions to the individual concerned about how to achieve these improvements.

   Discuss fully all questions which have not been given a 'yes' or 'no' response, again suggesting ways of improving things back at the workplace.

7   Give time checks at 30 and 45 minutes, renegotiating with syndicate groups if necessary. There are potentially 75 questions to be discussed. Some groups will find 30–45 minutes adequate. However, if all syndicate groups are gaining benefit from the analysis of the questionnaire, and if the overall timing of the course allows it, try to be flexible about renegotiating times.

8   Stop the syndicate group discussions after the agreed time. Lead a short plenary session, allowing individuals to share with the main group any important points which emerged from syndicate group discussions. Most, if not all participants will have discovered several issues which at the least will need clarification back at their place of work. Many will have identified areas where change is necessary. It would be useful if some of these issues were discussed in plenary so that individuals have the benefit of advice from the whole group.

9   Close the activity by issuing the Handout.

TRAINER NOTES

Leadership is a skill which, if not inherent in the individual, can be acquired through training, and by recognising the qualities and skills involved.

Some managers are born leaders. They have charisma – the sort of 'I would follow her / him anywhere' quality. Leadership for these individuals comes naturally. It is fine provided this attribute is used positively and subordinates are not exploited.

Other managers lead autocratically – from the front. If they have the respect of their teams and / or credibility through superior knowledge, this too can be a valid form of leadership.

Democratic leadership (within which is consultative and participative style leadership) encourages each member of the team to become involved in objective-setting, decision-making and so on, (while not abdicating overall responsibility for tasks, making decisions where necessary), and allows initiative and growth within the team. The democratic leader will inspire, encourage and generate commitment to the common objective.

No single style is appropriate for every situation. Each of these styles of leadership is valid and has its place. Autocratic leadership is essential in the armed forces for example. However, too often it is assumed that leadership of one sort or another is inherent in everyone. Because a person is a manager, it follows that she / he will be a good leader; training is not required. Unfortunately, this is not always the case.

This activity recognises that some participants will be 'naturals' but also that an essential part of any skill is to be aware of what that skill involves. By using a self-report questionnaire, individuals will be able to recognise the elements essential to effective leadership, and to rate their present competence as leaders. From this, they will be able to identify areas which need improving, information and guidance which needs to be obtained back at the workplace.

HANDOUT

Leadership skills involve achieving tasks against agreed objectives, and meeting the needs of the group or team as well as those of individuals within the team. To achieve a task the leader must know:

● where she / he is going
● how she / he is going to get there
● what is expected of each member of the team
● what she / he is doing

in order to complete the task efficiently and effectively using all the resources available

To meet individual / group / team needs a leader should:

● wherever possible involve the team in setting objectives, decision-making, problem-solving, progress / results review and revising objectives
● motivate and enthuse staff, clearly defining agreed objectives and targets
● ensure that good communication is maintained, up, down, and between all members of the team
● be approachable, but prepared to distance her / himself to resolve conflict, make decisions and use authority when or if the occasion demands it.

EXERCISE

Please answer yes or no to the following questions. If neither of these responses is appropriate, write a few words beneath the question, explaining your situation.

Getting the work done

1 Do I fully understand the current, organisational objectives of my firm?

_____

2 Am I kept informed / do I keep myself up to date with company policy and changes?

_____

3 Am I 100 per cent clear about my own responsibilities, accountabilities and degree of authority?

_____

4 Have I established long- and short-term objectives and targets for my team?

_____

5 Have I discussed and agreed these plans with my boss?

_____

6 Do I, and each member of my team have a clear idea about how these objectives are going to be met?

_____

7 Is there anyone on my team who is poorly motivated, or doesn't pull her / his weight?

_____

8 Could tasks be designed or redesigned to make the most of the talents and attributes of each individual of my team?

_____

9 Is our immediate working environment as good as it could be? (Think about layout, situation of telephones, lighting and so on.)

_____

10 Have I, and each person on my team got job specifications?

_____

11 Does everyone understand what their job is (not necessarily the same as 10 above)?

_____

12 Has each member of my team been given the opportunity to set her / his own targets and performance standards in consultation and agreement with me?

_____

13 Do I, and each member of my team, know to whom we are accountable?

_____

14 Do I keep my immediate superior appropriately informed?

_____

15 Do my team members keep me appropriately informed?

_____

16 Are there any gaps in my ability which could be improved by training?

_____

17 Are there gaps in any individual's performance which could be improved by in-house coaching, or external training?

_____

18 Could I improve my time management?

_____

19 Can each member of my team prioritise her / his workload to meet deadlines?

_____

20 As a team, are we meeting our objectives efficiently?

_____

21 As a team, are we meeting our objectives effectively?

_____

22 Am I clear about the difference between efficiency and effectiveness?

_____

23 While I'm on leave, do I make proper arrangements to ensure continuity of leadership?

_____

24 Have I made adequate provision for my absence during this training?

_____

25 Do I lead by example? Are my own standards of work and behaviour what I expect of my team?

_____

Use the space below for any observations from the group discussion to take place later.

_____

_____

_____

_____

_____

_____

Developing individuals in my team

1 Have I spoken with each individual about expected standards of performance?

_____

2 Does each individual understand her / his responsibilities *and* level of authority?

_____

3 Has everyone been informed of each of my team members' responsibilities and level of authority?

_____

4 Is each person clear about team and individual tasks and targets?

_____

5 Has each individual in my team the skill and experience to do her / his job with confidence?

_____

6 Have I got a record of every qualification gained and all training undertaken by each member of my team?

_____

7 Do I make use of these skills / areas of knowledge / expertise within the team?

_____

8 Do I conduct regular appraisal interviews with my team members to give feedback on progress and to include discussion of training or coaching needs?

_____

9 Does each person have adequate resources to do her / his job well?

_____

10 Is everyone (including me) aware of the need for training and possibly retraining to keep pace with change?

_____

11 Does anyone in my team resist change, even to the point of being obstructive?

_____

12 Do I acknowledge and praise success with the individual?

_____

13 Do I make individual successes public knowledge?

_____

14 Can I give constructive criticism when things go wrong?

_____

15 Do I help the individual solve her / his problems by offering guidance rather than *telling* her / him what to do, or putting matters right myself?

_____

16 Could I cut down on the amount of supervising / checking I do without losing control or authority?

_____

17 Could team members become more responsible for checking the accuracy and quality of their own work?

_____

18 Could more decision-making be done by individuals or the team without my involvement?

_____

19 Do individuals in my team sign *most* of their own letters?

_____

20 Are there individuals on my team who could answer queries / deal with aspects of my work as well as (or better than) I could?

_____

21 Is every individual's ability, aptitude and capacity matched by status and rewards (financial or non-financial)?

_____

22 Have I discussed career development with each of my team members?

_____

23 Is every member of my team clear about her / his own salary / career development?

_____

24 Do I know enough about each individual to be able to assess her / his attitudes to, and behaviour at work?

_____

25 Do I know and use the names of individuals' partners, children and so on in conversation?

_____

Use the space below for any observations arising from group discussion to take place later

_____

_____

_____

_____

_____

_____

_____

Team building

1 Do I recognise and understand the difference between work groups and teams?

_____

2 Do I agree that part of my role is to help meet both individual and team needs?

_____

3 Does the team know and understand organisational objectives, goals and policies?

_____

4 Does the team understand its role in relationship with other teams, sections or departments within the company?

_____

5 Have I discussed and agreed the team's targets and time-scales, allowing team members to set their own achievable, yet 'stretching' goals?

_____

6 Have I developed methods to monitor performance and measure results?

_____

7 Is the team clear about performance standards, quality, timekeeping and so on which I expect?

_____

8 Do I agree that sometimes it's best to 'lead from behind'?

_____

9 Do I agree that there may be occasions when I will have to 'lead from the front'?

_____

10 Do I look for opportunities to build teamwork into projects and tasks?

_____

11 Do I actively encourage interteam / interdepartmental communication and co-operation?

_____

12 Do I 'walk the job' to observe, listen to problems, praise progress and so on?

_____

13 Do I look out for things likely to disrupt the smooth working of the team, such as uneven workloads and so on?

_____

14 Do I intervene in the above instances rather than let the team solve its own problems?

_____

15 Do I hold regular, brief meetings to keep everyone in the picture about company policy, changes and so on?

_____

16 Does every team member feel _equally_ able to raise issues, offer suggestions, and speak freely?

_____

17 Do I consider conflict always to be an unhealthy aspect of team life?

_____

18 Do I take action to care for the well-being of the team and its working conditions?

_____

19 Am I prepared to represent the team and speak with its voice, on its behalf?

_____

20 Do I consult the team wherever possible, in decisions affecting its work?

_____

21 Do I always explain decisions I've made, thereby helping people to apply them?

_____

22 Do I welcome and encourage ideas and suggestions from the team?

_____

23 Can I encourage team initiative and autonomy without feeling threatened?

_____

24 Do my loyalties to the organisation and to the team ever conflict?

_____

25 Do I agree that however effective the team, I cannot abdicate responsibility for decision-making?

_____

4 Perceptions

Activity 18

• •

AS OTHERS SEE US

Description

Teams have the opportunity to assess individual members' strengths and weaknesses, transferable skills and attributes.

Aim

To maximise team effectiveness by recognising members' strengths and potential, and to identify possible areas for change, training or development.

Time

Variable, depending on size of work teams

Resources

- Sheet of flipchart paper and marker for each participant
- Means of attaching flipchart sheets to wall
- Flipchart and marker pen for trainer use
- Copy of Trainer notes

Method

1 Trainer input: to explain that this activity is about identifying individuals' strengths and weaknesses, as perceived by themselves – but also seen from others team members' perspectives. The activity calls for open and honest communication within work teams, and for constructive feedback, NOT negative or destructive views of self or others.

2 Participants must work with colleagues in their usual work teams for this activity, so divide into syndicate groups if necessary.

3 Issue a sheet of flipchart paper and marker to each participant. Display the previously prepared layout for the flipchart sheets (*see* Trainer notes). Participants should list skills and attributes – both in and out of the workplace. Explain that each section should be completed as honestly as possible. Instruct participants to complete their own sheets without consulting their colleagues at this stage (ten minutes).

4 Instruct group(s) to display their sheets where they can be easily seen by all team members (attached to a wall or on the floor).

5 If only one work team is represented, the processing of the activity can be trainer led. If the group was split into syndicate groups, ask each group to elect a leader (this does not have to be the workplace team leader).

6 Trainer input: to explain the procedure for processing the activity. The leaders (or trainer if participants did not split into syndicate groups) will 'run' the next part of the activity, encouraging all to give constructive feedback to the 'owner' of the sheet under discussion. Someone must volunteer to go first. That person should explain the reason for each inclusion on their sheet, uninterrupted. The team may then ask questions, make comments, add, clarify or amend as appropriate. For example, a team member may not have included an attribute – say 'generosity' for a number of reasons: modesty, embarrassment or they may not honestly consider themselves generous, yet others may see this quality and feel it should be included on that person's list. It may be that a negative quality has been omitted – again perhaps because that person hasn't considered that he or she is 'obstructive' at times, or 'moody'. Leaders must ensure that these negative features are handled sensitively and constructively, team members giving examples of behaviour which has been unhelpful, and offering positive feedback on how the situation might be improved.

It is usual for individuals to undervalue themselves. Team members should ensure that every positive skill and attribute is included on their colleague's sheet and should challenge any negative self-observation that they disagree with.

Every team member's sheet should be discussed. 10–15 minutes will be allowed for the analysis of each group member's sheet.

7 Begin the processing. If there is more than one group, circulate and observe closely to ensure that the constructive feedback rule is being complied with. Try to ensure that each participant's analysis ends on a positive note.

8 Reconvene the main group. Lead a short discussion on the activity.

Questions you might use:

- What are your feelings about this activity? Did you find it enlightening – or threatening for example? Did it dent your ego – or give you more self- confidence?
- Did anyone's list remain unaltered?
- Was anyone surprised at others' perceptions of them?
- In general terms, what did you discover about yourself . . . other people . . . your team?
- Was there a negative aspect to the activity?
- What were the main learning points of the activity?
- Did your team discover skills, attributes or hidden talents in members, previously unknown?
- Can you see an application for these skills etc in the workplace?
- Did you identify any training needs?

9 Ask each individual in turn what, if anything, they intend to change, or develop as a result of the activity. Stress the importance of identifying strengths and building on these, while recognising the need to change, modify or develop weaker areas.

10 Close the activity, thanking participants for their constructive discussions.

TRAINER NOTES

Participants will head up their sheets of flipchart paper as shown below. They are to list their own perceptions of their skills – both in and out of the workplace – and their positive and negative qualities.

SKILLS
I CAN . . . . .

POSITIVE QUALITIES	NEGATIVE QUALITIES
I AM	I AM . . . . .

Activity 19

IDEAS EXHIBITION

Description

An activity to be run early in the course, after introductions and an ice-breaker. Flipchart sheets are attached to the walls of the course room, each sheet bearing a different heading relevant to ideas central to the theme of the course – in this case, delivering quality service. Participants are free to add/amend ideas to any sheet at any time during the course. They should be encouraged to peruse the 'ideas exhibition' – rather like viewing exhibits in a gallery – before formal sessions and during breaks.

Aim

The sheets should help develop ideas, prompt new thoughts about the themes, and serve as a focus for the training. They will also be accurate indicators of the views of the group, and may show areas where more training needs to take place to achieve the overall objectives of the course. The sheets may also help the trainer to draw the various elements of the course together when summing up before the final evaluation session.

Time

Initially, 30 minutes; thereafter as necessary throughout the course.

Resources

- Sheets of flipchart paper
- Coloured marker for each participant
- Means of attaching flipchart paper to walls

Method

Some trainer preparation is required before beginning this activity. Sheets of flipchart paper should be attached to walls where they can be easily seen and worked on by participants. Each flipchart sheet will need to be headed by a question. Some examples are given (*see* Trainer notes) but each course will need to pose questions relevant to the training programme, the participating group(s) and the organisation(s) represented.

1 Trainer input: to explain that each flipchart sheet carries a different question relevant to the course. Participants will be asked to take a marker pen and visit each sheet in turn, adding their own comments or ideas to the list. They should avoid duplication. 15–30 minutes will be allowed for this. At the end of this time there will be a general discussion of the issues raised. After this initial stage, they should feel free to add to the list at any time during the course, and to consider the sheets during breaks. There will be the opportunity to review the lists later in the course.

2 Issue a marker pen to each participant. Instruct them to go and look at the sheets, adding their own comments beneath each question. They should feel free to discuss the issues raised by the questions with their colleagues. Depending on the number of sheets and number of participants, this should take from 15 to 30 minutes.

3 When ideas have been exhausted, ask participants to return to their seats. Take one sheet at a time and take feedback on each, adding any observations arising from these discussions, to the lists, if relevant.

4 Thank the group for their participation. Remind them that they should refer to the sheets throughout the course, adding and amending if necessary. (It may be advisable to ask whether additions or amendments have been made to lists at stages during the course, and to discuss as appropriate.)

5 Close this part of the activity by observing that the 'ideas exhibition' has hopefully helped participants focus on the main themes and issues of the course, and will be used as a reference throughout the training programme.

6 (Optional) Use the sheets to help sum up at the end of the course.

7 Close the activity.

TRAINER NOTES

The concept of the 'ideas exhibition' can be used for any training event; any questions can be posed on any theme relevant to particular training programmes.

Here we are suggesting it be used for training in quality management, or customer care. The following are examples of headings for your flipchart sheets. It is not suggested you use all of these, or that you use this wording. This is only to give some indication of the sort of issues which may get participants thinking. You will obviously need to include issues relevant to your specific training programme and to the group(s) and organisation(s) represented.

The questions should include areas which help participants identify their own role as internal customers, their relationship with other parts of the chain within the organisation, the impact on the external user and the overall necessity for quality service by every link in the chain.

- What do you understand by the term 'customer care'? What does it involve?
- Who are our external customers?
- Who are our internal customers?
- What do our customers want from us?
- Who supplies us?
- What do we need of our suppliers?
- Is there a discrepancy between what our suppliers say / think they do, and what is actually delivered in terms of product or service?
- What are the elements involved in delivering quality?
- What are the advantages of quality management for organisations?
- What are the implications of quality management for organisations?
- What are the implications of quality management for us?

NB You may need to clarify terminology, and to explain, for example, that 'suppliers' could mean external suppliers – of raw materials, consultancy, etc. – or internal suppliers; who provides you with stationery, or who makes the gromple that you have to weld to the scutcheon?

It may also be necessary to give one or two examples under each heading to get things started, and / or to add your own observations if there are glaring omissions. Under the heading 'What do you understand by the term "customer care" what does it involve?' for example, possible responses could include:

- meeting the needs of the customer
- showing respect for the customer
- providing quality service
- providing the best possible product in the fastest possible time
- excellent after-sales service
- making efficient use of resources

and so on.

Under 'What are the advantages of quality management for organisations?' possible responses might be:

- profitability
- innovative approaches
- job security
- striving to be the best
- everyone accountable

and so on.

Activity 20

• •

CUSTOMERS: THEM AND US

Description

An activity to identify each group's/individual's customers, both inside and outside the organisation, from immediate colleagues to end users; also, contacts of whom *they* are customers.

Aim

To show that the term 'customer' includes everyone to whom managers and staff supply a product or service, and that customer care involves delivering quality service to all these contacts.

Time

1 hour – 1 hour 30 minutes

Resources

- Flipchart paper and marker pen for each syndicate group
- Means of attaching flipchart paper to wall

Method

1 Trainer input: to explain that the term 'customer' is often taken to mean just the end user of a product or service, e.g. the person who buys the compact disk player, or the client of a solicitor, or the patient in a hospital. This definition can be expanded to include any person or group who interacts with an organisation and whose well-being is of concern to that organisation.

This would include suppliers *to* the organisation, and suppliers *of* the product or service (if this involves a chain to the end-user) e.g. few manufacturers sell directly to the public, but supply retailing outlets. The 'customers' of the manufacturer, in this context, are all the organisations in the retail chain, plus the end-user – the person who purchases the goods and takes them home.

There are also customers within each organisation. Employees in other departments or sections may also be your 'customers'. It may be that one department cannot function without products or services supplied by another internal department – in fact, it's almost certain that every section of an organisation is interdependent on another or others. It follows that the quality each department can deliver depends on the quality offered by its providers.

It also follows that if colleagues or departments within the organisation are our customers, we too can be seen as customers to them. If we deliver inferior service to them, their work suffers as a result.

Customer care involves far more than looking to the needs of the end-user; it means recognising just who all customers are, and delivering a quality service with every transaction inside and outside the organisation.

2 Explain that the purpose of this activity is first to identify customers in the context of participants' own working environments, second to establish what, in terms of product or service, is supplied in each case, and third to ascertain where and how improvements might be made.

3 If necessary, divide the group into smaller syndicate groups. It is important that each group comprises people with similar roles within the organisation.

4 Issue a sheet of flipchart paper and marker to each group. Instruct groups to divide the paper into six sections (*see* Trainer notes). Groups are to work together to complete the three sections *Customers – Internal, Customers – External,* and *Customers – Us.* Allow up to 30 minutes for this.

5 It may be necessary to circulate between groups to help get them started. They should consider *everyone* for whom they provide a service within or outside the organisation, as customers, and include them on their lists. (It may be helpful to start from the end-user, and work backwards.) The third section on the left-hand side of the sheet should be a list of people/departments/sections/suppliers etc who provide them with a service, i.e. to whom they are customers and require quality care.

6 Ask groups to pin up their lists where the whole group can see them. Ask a spokesperson/scribe from each group in turn to talk through their list, completing the right-hand sections as they do so. This entails writing against each identified 'customer' the type of product or service supplied in each case. This will involve both conferring with the syndicate, and discussion and input from the whole group. Questioning and probing should be encouraged, and may well produce additional 'customers' to add to each syndicate's list.

7 When all groups have completed their lists, lead a general discussion on how satisfactory all identified transactions with customers are felt to be.

Questions you might use:

- Where could there be improvements?
- What would have to happen to effect these improvements?
- Where are the possible pitfalls? How could these be overcome?
- Who needs to be consulted?
- Who needs to be informed?
- What additional resources would be needed? How might these needs be met?

It is probable that during the latter stages of this activity, participants may identify reasons (or excuses) for not providing a better service. These reasons may well include the fact that others within the organisation or external suppliers provide them with perceived inferior products or services. It is important to process this fully (Step 7). You may need to explore where and how changes might be made to the benefit of individuals/sections, the organisation and the end-user. Actively discourage 'scapegoating' by concentrating on how things might be improved rather than dwelling on problems that exist.

8 Close the activity by asserting the need to recognise all customers' requirements in order to deliver quality service.

TRAINER NOTES

Instruct groups to divide their sheet of flipchart paper into six, as shown, and to head the left-hand boxes CUSTOMERS – INTERNAL, CUSTOMERS – EXTERNAL, and CUSTOMERS – US. An example of the sort of responses to expect has been given for your guidance. This example represents the responses of a semi-skilled operative working for a company which produces engineering components for aircraft fuel systems.

CUSTOMERS – INTERNAL	
Jack and Stan	Check for flaws – finish. De-burr threads of socket sleeves.
Assembly-line workers	Put components together to form sub-assembly.
Inspectors	Check sub-assemblies.
Test engineers	Test assemblies for malfunctions.
CUSTOMERS – EXTERNAL	
Carnells	Buy components.
Whitney Engines	Buy sub-assemblies.
Travelling public } Servicemen/women	Travel in aircraft using engines which have our components / assemblies / fuel systems.
CUSTOMERS – US	
Machine operator	Makes basic components.
Marcia – engineer	Sets specifications for basic components.
Bond storeman	Stores raw materials.
Jarrets	Supplies raw materials (sometimes faulty).
Payroll department	
Personnel	

Activity 21

. . . .

QUALITY

Description

A group activity designed to help participants reflect on the meaning of quality and its implications for customer care. It would be of benefit if participants already understand the term 'customer' to mean everyone in the chain, internal and external, to whom a product or service is offered.

Aim

To demonstrate that 'quality' is not necessarily synonymous with 'excellence' and that value to a customer will not be solely determined by a superior product or service at the moment of delivery

Time

1 hour

Resources

- Notepaper and pencils/pens
- Flipchart and marker pen for trainer use

Method

1 Trainer input: to explain to the group that quality means different things to different people at different times and in different situations. However, within organisations there must be a clear understanding that quality means meeting the requirements of the customer. (*see* Trainer notes 1 for further guidance.)

2 Tell participants that, as a group(s) they will attempt to define 'quality'. In order to put the concept into a context, they will imagine that they are going to purchase a new photocopier. They will discuss what criteria should be used to choose between competitive manufacturers and providers of photocopying equipment. They should consider, for example, what questions should be put to competitors for comparison, and having made the choice, what features of the service offered by the chosen company constitute 'quality' customer care.

3 If appropriate, divide participants into small groups. Issue notepaper and pencils. Instruct them to decide on major headings for consideration in obtaining this 'quality' product and service. If they have difficulty getting started, give them one or two headings from the list – *see* Trainer notes 2. Allow 30 minutes for this.

4 After 30 minutes, draw up a composite list on flipchart paper. You could either ask the group for their headings, discussing reasons for their decision to include each item as you go, or use Trainer notes 2 as a guide.

5 If you chose the first option, use Trainer notes 2 to supplement the group's headings, and add any thoughts of your own to complete the list.

6 If you have not already done so at Steps 4 or 5, discuss details involved under each of the headings, outlined in Trainer notes 2.

7 Close the activity by concluding that 'quality' involves far more than the specific performance of a product or service. What is looked for in other providers – in this case, suppliers of photocopiers – should also be given to users of the participants' product or service. In order to define 'quality' in the context of the group's own sphere of work, the first step is always to clarify the full requirements of the customer.

TRAINER NOTES 1

Which is the quality product, a Rolls Royce or a Mini? The answer, of course, is that both *can* be – it depends on why you want the product in the first place. If you want comfort and roominess, luxurious upholstery, high performance and so on, a Rolls Royce would fit the bill. If, however, you need an economical town car – nippy and easy to park – you would be foolish to consider a Rolls Royce; a Mini would better suit your needs. What *is* important is that, in terms of quality, you choose the best in the range to fit your criteria.

So what are the factors you would consider? What denotes 'quality'? Take the case of the economical town car. You would need to consider value for money in terms of the product itself, and therefore compare similar small cars for performance, comfort, added extras and so on. You would need to look at reliability – perhaps consult consumer magazines – to ascertain 'quality' in these terms. Then there is the question of availability – not just of the car itself, but of parts; which brings us to the issue of after-sales services. The list goes on and on.

Quality, therefore, is not just a matter of the end-product or service offered to the consumer, but the way an entire organisation or operation is managed. Top quality can only be delivered if all requirements of the customer are met, and met in a way superior to that offered by competitors.

TRAINER NOTES 2

What elements are involved in providing a quality product or service?

Example: Purchasing a photocopier

What type of machine / service

Do you need a machine which prints back to back; on A3 and A4 size paper; in black and white or in colour; which reduces or enlarges; which has an ink cassette or a drum? Does it have to fit on a desk or can it be free-standing? Do you need a collating feature . . . and so on.

Staff

Initial enquiries will mean communicating with a telephonist, receptionist and / or sales staff of the competing companies. What is the first impression? Are they polite, helpful, considerate, professional, informative, friendly?

Price

Needs to be competitive. This does not necessarily mean cheapest. High standards of materials, workmanship etc. required comparing favourably with others of similar price.

Value for money

This includes added extras (not offered for a similar price by competitors) and also the hidden extras such as after-sales service.

Reliability

How does it compare with similar makes? What is the average number of call-outs per year for breakdowns. Is it high tech or user friendly?

Delivery time

Is this a crucial factor? Can the company guarantee delivery time and date? Can the company agree to install at a time and date convenient to you?

Materials

Can the firm provide paper, ink, cassettes and so on? Are their rates competitive? What sort of notice is required?

Installation

Appearance of engineers – are they polite, smart, appropriately dressed? Do they conform to your company rules (e.g. non-smoking policies etc.)? Are they self-sufficient in terms of tools, equipment, materials? Are they efficient and professional in approach?

Customer training

Are instruction manuals well written, easy to follow and jargon free? What training is given to the customer on use and maintenance of the machine?

Guarantees and service contracts

How long is the item fully guaranteed? What items are included / excluded in service contracts? How much does the service contract cost each year?

After-sales service

In case of breakdown, what is the average response time? Is there an efficient mechanism for reporting faults so that engineers arrive prepared (i.e. do they carry necessary parts / equipment to carry out repairs)? Is the company eager to correct faults as quickly as possible with as little cost and inconvenience as possible? Does the same fault recur? Generally, how are complaints handled?

These are some – not all – of the elements which make up quality service and good customer care. Most of these headings can be adapted to meet every work situation, and should be applied when considering delivering quality to customers, whether they are internal colleagues / departments, suppliers, or end- users and consumers.

Activity 22

IMAGE

Description

An activity which looks at the quality demanded by discerning customers of various services and organisations, and at the importance of image in winning and keeping customers.

Aim

Using a case study which is not work related, participants will consider customer care in a non-threatening way, and be able to apply the general principles learned to their own work situations.

Time

1 hour – 1 hour 30 minutes

Resources

- Copy of the Exercise for each participant
- Notepaper, pens/pencils
- Flipchart and marker pen for trainer use

Method

1 Divide participants into syndicate groups of three or four if necessary. Issue a copy of the exercise (a case study) to each participant, and notepaper and pens/pencils for group use.

2 Explain that participants are to put themselves in the place of a young family which is going on a day's outing to celebrate their young son's birthday. They will travel to the town centre by bus, visit a large department store to buy a toy for their son, then go to a burger bar for lunch. The task of the group is to look at each area – public transport, retail store and fast food outlet, and decide what each should be providing to meet customer needs. Groups should make lists on the notepaper. After 30 minutes the groups will share their findings in plenary, and a compilation list will be drawn up on a flipchart.

3 Begin the exercise. After the allotted time, ask for a spokesperson from each group to read out the elements agreed to be necessary for good customer care in each of the areas – bus, store and burger bar. Record the elements on a flipchart.

4 Discuss any issues raised and refine list as necessary. Add any thoughts of your own (*see* Trainer notes). At this point you could begin to highlight areas which are pertinent to your own work situation.

5 Ask participants to take some time to look at the list from the perspective of their own working environment. For example, can they see any relevance to their own response to customer care? Where could improvements be made? Lead a short discussion on issues raised.

6 Sum up by suggesting individuals copy the list into the space provided on the case study sheet, and to use the list to revise their own, their department's and their organisation's practices.

7 Close the activity.

✎ EXERCISE

Tom and Jenny have two small children – Ben who is six today and Sophie who is just ten months old. The family is going to travel by bus to the town centre, visit a department store to buy a toy for Ben's birthday. They plan to have lunch at a burger bar.

Under three headings – BUS, STORE, and BURGER BAR – list what the family might be looking for in terms of quality service and good customer care.

Bus

_____

_____

_____

_____

_____

_____

Store

_____

_____

_____

_____

_____

_____

Burger bar

_____

_____

_____

_____

_____

_____

TRAINER NOTES

Some possible inclusions:

Bus

- user friendly timetable at bus stop
- adequate bus shelter
- frequency of buses
- punctuality of buses
- clarity of destination information on buses
- sufficient buses to meet client needs
- sufficient seating to meet client needs
- seats for disabled / mothers with small children etc
- sufficient space for parcels
- cleanliness
- appearance of driver / conductor
- politeness of driver / conductor
- skill of driver
- helpfulness of driver / conductor
- driver / conductor knowledge of services / connections etc
- how conflict is handled

Store

- adequate in-store signs
- accessibility of escalators, lifts
- accessibility of toy department
- logical layout of department
- attractive layout of department
- clean carpets etc., dust-free shelves and merchandise
- wide variety of goods on accessible display
- hands-on samples – opportunity for children to try toys
- sufficient well-informed, trained staff
- salespeople who do not try to sell you what you don't want / need
- helpful guidance about product range

- advice on suitability of toy – will it meet the need?
- appearance and attitude of salespeople – IMAGE!
- easy payment / credit facilities
- assurance of immediate replacement if toy proves faulty
- competitive pricing
- availability of product – sample toy on display is in stock
- speed of obtaining out of stock item
- assurance of telephone / letter communication immediately the product becomes available
- telephone instruction if there is a hitch in the ordering
- sufficient seating in department (for parents while children play, for example)
- toilet facilities nearby
- baby changing area

Burger bar

- cleanliness
- easy to read menus
- speed of service
- attitude of staff
- appearance of staff
- different staff handling / serving food and taking money
- quality of food
- quantity of food
- value for money – competitive with other similar bars
- choice of food
- attractiveness of food presentation
- freshly cooked produce
- children's menu
- special features for children
- eating environment – right temperature – relaxed atmosphere – adequate room between tables – décor
- comfortable seating
- sufficient seating
- quickly cleared / cleaned tables

- piped music – appropriate? volume?
- customer satisfaction questionnaire
- anyone check that everything is satisfactory?
- toilet facilities
- baby changing facilities.

Activity 23

....

PERSPECTIVES

Description

When it is necessary for someone to try to change the attitude or behaviour of another, personal beliefs, expectations and needs often override a consideration of the other person's viewpoint; conflict and resistance can be the result. This activity suggests a format for planning meetings where such changes are required, and aims at motivating rather than unwittingly erecting barriers to progress. It should be run in conjunction with, and prior to the activity 'Plan for Progress'.

Aim

To encourage participants to identify and consider the views of those involved when negotiating for improvement.

Time

1 hour

Resources

- Flipchart and marker pen for trainer use
- Copy of Exercise for each participant
- Copy of Handout for each participant
- Means of attaching flipchart sheets to wall

Method

1 Trainer input: to introduce the activity. There will be times in the working life of everyone when someone with whom they have to deal has their own problems with work (inefficiency etc.), with attitude (interpersonal skills, resistance to change) or with behaviour (inappropriate). The activity addresses this by suggesting the use of careful forward planning, to include not only the needs and expectations of the team, but consideration for the individual concerned. By trying to establish her/his fears, goals, needs and drives, a suitable approach can be adopted, and success achieved with harmony rather than hostility, resentment and resistance to the changes you propose. The exercise asks participants to consider a situ-

ation where one person (a finance officer) is causing real problems for one of their internal customers, in this case the head of another department.

2 Issue Exercise which is a hypothetical scenario from which the group will initially work. In order for participants to understand the principles suggested by this activity, you should take participants through the various stages, using the scenario as an example.

3 Allow participants about five minutes to read the scenario.

4 Trainer input: to explain why forethought is important before embarking on an exchange similar to the one about to take place in the scenario. Before any formal communication, it is important to plan the proceedings with care. It is so easy to let emotions rule, to rush into the situation and end up antagonising the other person. The results of such a meeting will inevitably be counter-productive. It is also very easy (and human) to see things only from one's own perspective.

5 The group will now analyse the situation presented, and make some assumptions about the needs and feelings of the protagonists, Ted and Lois. Using a flipchart, examine the situation from Ted's point of view first. Begin with his goals.

   Steps 5, 6 and 7 will take about 15 minutes together. Head the sheet 'What Ted Wants'. Ask participants to consider Ted's objective goals. He has just set up another meeting with Lois. What results does he want?

   List ideas as they are called out by the group, discussing as you go issues which may be raised (or which can be included if not raised by the group). Ted wants:

   - financial reports to be accurate
   - financial reports to be on time
   - to be sure that Lois understands what Ted requires of her
   - to avoid having to have such encounters with her every term
   - for Lois to be more responsible for her actions.

(If the truth be known, Ted also probably wants to hear that Lois has resigned!)

6 Make another list, this time of Ted's needs and feelings. Needs are more difficult to define, because they are about emotions and feelings, and will necessarily be more subjective. Head this section 'What Ted Feels' and ask the group to empathise with Ted and suggest some of his probable feelings at this time. These could include:

- I don't want the stress of being unsure of my figures
- I don't want to be made look a fool in front of the rector again
- I don't want to upset Lois
- Why can't Lois adopt my own high standards?
- I don't want another confrontation which damages the relationships between the academic staff and the administrative team
- I might be judged by Lois's poor standards
- This is my third attempt with Lois. My authority is suffering
- She is getting increasingly hostile. I dread meetings with her
- I don't want the rector to think I can't sort out problems like this
- I would be happier if I did the job myself next term!

7   Make a third and final list headed 'Ted's Expectations'. This time, using the information you have about previous encounters with Lois, deduce the sort of expectations Ted might have of the outcome of yet another meeting. Issues which might arise include:

- I'll intend to be firm but fair
- She'll clam up and become more sullen than ever
- I'll get really angry and become aggressive
- She'll make excuses – blame other members of the team, or the computer, or unco-operative teaching staff, or pressure of work because of her boss's absence – anything but take the blame herself
- She'll try to put the blame on me – 'it was alright in the old days; nothing went wrong then; you're too fussy' and so on
- I'll threaten
- She'll apologise and say it won't happen again
- I'll end up doing the report myself

8   Pin these lists to the wall, where they can be easily seen by the group. Make similar lists for Lois, beginning with 'What Lois Wants'.

Steps 8, 9 and 10 will take about 15 minutes together. Ask participants to now try to look at the situation from Lois's point of view. Enough information is provided for an educated guess at what *any* Lois might be feeling as she prepares for another meeting with Ted. Try to identify with her to decide, first, what she wants from the meeting. Issues which may arise might include:

- want to avoid a scene
- want to keep my job
- want him to recognise that I need help
- want to be given the means to do an efficient job
- want to get my reports right, and in on time

9 Write another list for Lois's needs. Make a list for the second area – to look at 'What Lois Feels'. Issues which might arise are:

- need to feel I'm not a failure
- feel guilty because I know my work is not perfect
- feel resentful that I can't help it; times have moved on and I've not moved with them, but it's not my fault
- feel angry that I'm chastised but not offered help
- feel ashamed that I can't admit I'm floundering, and ask for help
- need to still feel part of a valued team
- need to save face with my colleagues.

10 Write a third list for Lois under the heading 'Lois's Expectations'. From her experiences of the previous two meetings with Ted, ask participants to describe what Lois's expectations of this third meeting are likely to be:

- I'd like to be honest, but I'll get defensive, then aggressive
- He'll shout and get irritated with me
- He'll demand better quality work from me
- He won't accept any excuses
- I'll end up apologising and promising to do better, but not knowing how to improve
- I'll leave his office feeling a failure.

11 Pin Lois's corresponding lists beside Ted's so that they can be easily compared. Pin Ted's 'wants' next to Lois's 'wants', his 'feelings' next to hers, and so on, ensuring that the lists can be seen by all participants.

12 Ask for initial reactions from the group. It should be clear that both lists centre around the self. Ted sees the situation almost entirely from his point of view, as does Lois. Neither considers the other's needs in this matter. Ask the group if this is typical, and whether they can relate this to similar situations in which they have been involved.

13 Using the lists as 'evidence', suggest ways in which the expected outcome of the meeting could be altered.

Questions you might use:

- Why is there a communication breakdown?
- Who is to blame?
- Whose responsibility is it to initiate a discussion of the *real* problems?
- What are the key issues as demonstrated by this scenario?
- At the coming meeting, what approach could Ted use to change the outcome predicted by his 'expectations' as listed?
- What could Lois do to stop herself conforming to her stereotypical behavioural patterns?
- How important is the 'face-saving' element in such encounters?
- What can Ted do to achieve the results he requires of Lois, while making her feel valued and good about herself?

14 Trainer input: to suggest that, when faced with a situation where the behaviour or attitude of a colleague needs modification, a bit of forethought, and the drawing up of lists such as those above, would be a good way to plan for the meeting. It is easy to draw up a list of personal wants, goals, feelings, needs, emotions, and expectations. Writing a similar list for the other person is not so easy and relies on hard evidence, but also assumptions drawn from a knowledge of that person, their reactions on similar occasions, a knowledge of human behaviour in general terms, and most importantly through observation and empathy – trying to put yourself in their shoes for a while. This 'evidence' needs to be checked out at the meeting, while trying to tease out the real issues involved and finding mutually agreeable and acceptable solutions.

The whole process of using charts and writing lists under the headings suggested, a) clarifies the situation, b) establishes previous behaviour patterns on both sides which contributed to blockages, and c) enables progress by seeing the issues not just as product or service problems, but as 'person' issues, to be solved by improved communication and understanding of the other's feelings, needs and perspectives.

15 Issue Handout. If any of the points raised in this handout have not been discussed, look at these now.

16 Close the activity.

(Although this activity can stand alone, the learning is reinforced if the Activity 'Plan for Progress' is now run. It uses the learning points from this activity, and applies them to examples from participants' own working life.)

EXERCISE

Ted has recently been appointed vice-principal of a small college. This is his third academic term. His appointment resulted from the college's growth in size and status, and recent amalgamation with a group of colleges, all reporting to a central administration unit headed by Giles West, the rector.

Ted has to have regular dealings with Lois, who is the college finance officer. She has been in post for several years, and is office manager as well as being in charge of finance for the college. Part of her role has always been to provide departments with a regular analysis of their expenditure and commitments. A copy of all these reports, in a composite form, now also goes to Ted, who sees himself as an internal customer of Lois's finance section.

Lois has made no secret of her resentment of recent changes, especially the introduction of computers networked to a minicomputer at headquarters. Her bookkeeping methods had always sufficed in the past, but she was now required to work with spreadsheets and financial software.

At the end of his first term, the autumn session, there were major errors in Lois's financial report to Ted. He, in turn, (and unwittingly) presented this erroneous report to the rector. Ted had been extremely embarrassed by this, especially as the errors were revealed at a meeting of the Academic Board. He had spoken with Lois accordingly, leaving her in no doubt of his dissatisfaction.

The second term was worse, with lecturers now complaining about lack of payment because of errors originating from the college office. There were mix–ups over student grant payments, and again, errors in the termly financial report. Luckily, this time they were found, by Ted, in advance of the Academic Board meeting. Unfortunately, the extent of the errors meant a late report, and the postponement of the meeting as a result. This time Ted really had a go at Lois, telling her she was going to have to 'pull up her socks' or else he would have to formally report her to the college registrar (Lois's boss). Ted had, of course, already spoken with the registrar but had not then wished to make an issue of it, hoping he could resolve matters with Lois without formal complaint.

This third term is the most important, but Lois is in difficulties again. The college registrar is on prolonged sick leave and Lois is in sole charge of finance. Heads of department had been told that there were no funds left – in fact an over-spending was apparent – but then a significant error was discovered, by one of Lois's junior colleagues, in Lois's calculations. The result was that, with just a few weeks to go, the college has to spend a large sum of money, or lose it back to the 'system'. The financial situation is chaotic. Ted's draft financial report is due, and there is every indication that Lois will miss the deadline again.

Ted decides he cannot avoid another meeting with her, as he cannot wait for the registrar to return.

HANDOUT

Tips for forming a communication strategy

1 List your own goals, targets, needs, feelings and expectations under the following headings: What I want; What I feel; My expectations.

2 Make three similar lists for the person with whom you intend to communicate.

3 Compare the lists, point by point, looking for areas of similarity. You will probably find mainly areas of differences.

4 Look for ways in which the expected outcome can be improved. How can stereotypical behaviour, on both sides, be modified?

The following checklist might help.

● Try to be succinct. Make specific statements rather than vague generalisations. Look for evidence to back up these statements. This helps turn subjective feelings and ideas into facts on which you can work.

● Be honest about your own emotions and needs. Recognise and acknowledge these as an integral part of the communication process.

● Attempt to establish what the other person logically needs. Put yourself in their shoes. Use your perception to establish what you, or anyone, would want to happen in their situation. This can be checked out at the meeting with carefully prepared questions, and offers of assistance of a kind acceptable to you both.

● Imagine their expectations of the coming meeting, and preempt this by adopting a different approach. Instead of showing your irritation, count to ten, state the problem as you see it, open new avenues for discussion, use humour and so on to defuse the situation, look for ways forward.

● If you've guessed their assessment of the situation, but don't do what's expected, you're more likely to gain and keep their attention, and turn resistance into co-operation.

5 Quality standards

Activity 24

· ·

RIGHT FIRST TIME

Description

This activity looks at the cost of errors to individuals, departments and organisations.

Aim

To demonstrate that errors waste time, that wasted time means wasted resources, and that abuse of time and resources can lose goodwill and/or business.

Time

1 hour 30 minutes

Resources

- Copy of Exercise for each participant

Method

1 Trainer input: many organisations still use quality assurance through post-production testing. Inspectors are employed to ensure that goods or services leaving the premises meet product standards. Those meeting standards – which conform to preordained customer requirements – are released; those which don't go for scrap, are reworked, sold on as 'seconds' or are returned for correction.

This institutionalised waste is the quality inspectors' output. The inspectors' continued employment depends on a proportion of faulty goods getting through the system.

Increasingly, large and small businesses are adopting Total Quality Management (TQM). One of the facets of this is the 'right first time' concept, whereby individuals take responsibility for their own areas of work – of getting it right first time – and don't rely on faults being picked up later through the inspection process. This decreases the occurrence of failures and rejects. The cost of not getting it right first time can be considerable in terms of money and resources.

This activity uses case studies to demonstrate the cost of errors in the workplace – and to individuals working alone.

2 Issue a copy of the Exercise to each participant. If necessary, divide the group into pairs/triads or small syndicate groups. They should discuss each of the scenarios presented (45 minutes).

3 In the main group, discuss any issues which arose from the case studies, paying particular attention to question 4 which relates the learning to individuals' own work situations.

4 Close the activity.

EXERCISE

List the cost in terms of time and resources in the following scenarios:

1 Anne is a hairdresser. In a few minutes, one of her more fastidious customers is due to arrive to have highlights put into her hair. Anne goes to the store cupboard to collect the chemicals she needs and discovers that a box of Oxidant which she thought was full, is in fact empty. She hasn't the hydrogen peroxide she needs for the first stage of the treatment. She hurriedly writes a note for one of the juniors to take to the supplier:

'One box Oxidant to mix with Fairway powder bleach. Please invoice.'

The junior hurries off to the supplier – about ten minutes drive away.

'What volume peroxide does she want?' the supplier asks.

'She didn't say; the usual I suppose. It's for highlights.'

'Well I don't know – we'd better check on the Fairway powder box. That'll tell us.'

The supplier goes to his storeroom and returns to the front counter with the box of powder bleach. 'It says here 20 per cent volume for general use or 30 per cent for higher degree of lift. What do you think – the general use? Shall we go for the 20 per cent?'

'I'm not sure. Perhaps I could phone the shop from here, and check?'

The phone is engaged, and continues to be so.

'I'll risk the 20 per cent I think. Will you change it if it's wrong?'

'Of course. I'll go and get the box of 20 per cent volume for you. Will you wait while I write out an invoice please.'

The junior returns to the shop, 30 minutes later. The client has been prepared and has been sitting for 15 minutes waiting for her treatment to begin. Anne looks with dismay at the peroxide.

'Didn't I ask for 30 per cent volume? I have to use 30 per cent on Mrs ..... the 20 per cent won't touch her hair!'

2 Jean has recently had a bereavement in the family, and has taken time off from work for the funeral and to be with her parents. This was immediately followed by a period of sick leave. Now back at work, she has just received her payslip for the relevant month, and finds that she has had large deduc-

tions made from her salary. She had expected full pay for her sick leave, and compassionate leave for the bereavement, but has been stopped several days' pay.

Jean works for a large organisation in the service sector. She is part of one of three small project teams; Tom is her project team leader. The section manager is Sarah Long.

Jean took her payslip immediately to Tom and spoke at length with him about her grievance. Although he commiserated with Jean, there was nothing he could do to put matters right, so she has now made an appointment to speak with Sarah about it.

3 On being made redundant, Jim decides to try his hand at writing magazine articles. Although in no way computer literate – and not wanting to be – Jim decides that investing some of his redundancy money in a word processor would be a worthwhile venture. Excited at the prospect, and eager to start, Jim takes a trip to his local computer store.

The assistants are all young computer buffs who seem more interested in selling games machines to their peer group than in advising Jim. On eventually securing the attention of one, and explaining that he wanted to buy a word processor, this assistant says that he can't really offer any suggestions – best to speak to the manager, whom he calls.

The manager learns of Jim's lump sum, and questions him about his new career plans. He has just the machine for Jim – a demonstration personal computer which he could let him have at a special discount. It was just three months old, and came with a printer and basic word processing software. Could he also interest Jim in one of the best, most widely used business databases at half price – an unrepeatable offer – and Jim would surely need to set up a database in the future.

Jim agrees – well, he'll soon learn how to make the best of his purchases, and the manager assures him that it is all very easy and straightforward. He arranges payment and agrees to collect his equipment at the weekend. On collection, Jim sees that he has been given a £10.00 voucher – not as a free gift, but in lieu of the user manual for the machine which had been mislaid.

With the help of a friend, Jim manages to connect everything satisfactorily and after an initial whirring and clicking the monitor produces a blank screen with the letter 'C' in the top left-hand corner. Whatever Jim does to the keyboard, nothing happens – the 'C' stays unblinkingly and irritatingly there.

After several abortive phone calls to the shop, Jim eventually manages to speak to the manager, who talks him through the basics of installing the disk operating system.

Over the next three weeks, and after countless calls to the shop, Jim's computer was eventually up and running. He enjoyed writing his first article, and looked forward to seeing it in print. He tried. Nothing! Another phone call to the shop. 'Have you checked your Dip Switches?' asked the manager. 'My WHAT?' Finally, after much explanation, the printer actually printed something – a page full of hieroglyphics! Another phone call during which the manager talked Jim through locating and checking the printer driver, and the article appeared in all its faint dot-matrix glory!

The article was accepted – 'Why not write a regular diary slot? You'll need to buy a modem to download your material to the editorial department'. More visits and phone calls to the shop, after which Jim knew all about Hayes compatibility, protocols and jumpers, but was resentful because he didn't WANT to know about these things – he just wanted a system which worked.

More writing success, and the publishers want Jim to include graphics. Back to the shop. 'You need a scanner and a word processor capable of basic desktop publishing. You should have bought a different computer with extra RAM to accommodate the GUI' he was told. Jim doesn't bother to ask what a GUI is – just reaches for his wallet.

The good news is that the GUI comes with a card-index program, so Jim never did need to learn how to operate his database. The bad news is that his scanned images looked fine on the monitor, but dreadful when printed with his dot-matrix printer. What a pity he hadn't bought a laser printer...

4 Share with your colleagues any incidents which have occurred/continue to occur at your own place of work where insufficient or incorrect information leads to waste of time or resources.

Can you think of many instances where faulty materials or workmanship have resulted in a waste of time or resources for a number of people?

What measures could be taken to eliminate such errors? Why are these measures not taken at present? How could management and employees be encouraged to 'get it right first time' in their areas of work?

TRAINER NOTES

Questions you might use to facilitate discussion:

Scenario 1

- What has been the *real* cost to Anne's business? (*Her, her junior's and the supplier's time – and time is money; cost of petrol; goodwill of customer; stress for all concerned.*)
- What is wrong with the salon's ordering system?
- What else might Anne have done to avert this crisis? (*Might have phoned the order through to the supplier so that it was ready for collection by junior.*)

Scenario 2

- What are the costs in terms of time and resources?
- Was it appropriate for Jean to go to her team leader with this matter? (*Only for a sympathetic ear; not for action.*)
- Assuming that Jean works for a large organisation, to whom should she have gone with her queries? (*Payroll clerk; head of accounts; personnel; welfare.*)

Scenario 3

- What has it cost Jim in terms of time and resources?
- If you had been in Jim's position, what might you have done initially to avoid his ensuing problems? (*Plan his present and future needs; read magazines; consult computer literate colleagues; go to recommended sources; shop around etc.*)
- What action might Jim have taken at subsequent stages to make his life a little easier? (*Cut losses with shop; do any or all of the above.*)
- How could the shop manager have helped Jim avoid his problems? (*Listened to Jim / helped to identify his needs at the outset; offered to set up and install the hardware and software.*)

Activity 25
••
HAPPINESS SHEET

Description

The best way of assessing customers' needs is to ask them. Whether, and to what extent, these needs are met needs constantly to be reviewed. This can be done in a number of ways – personally or by telephone, or by devising surveys or customer satisfaction questionnaires. This activity examines the elements needed to compile an effective customer satisfaction questionnaire.

Aim

To enable participants to understand the benefits and limitations of customer satisfaction questionnaires by discussing principles and criteria, and by compiling a questionnaire for their own client groups.

Time

1 hour 30 minutes – 2 hours

Resources

- Notepaper and pens/pencils
- Flipchart paper and markers
- Means of attaching flipchart sheets to wall
- Flipchart and marker for trainer use
- (Optional) Copies of Trainer notes to issue as Handouts

Method

1 Trainer input: to explain the appropriateness of using customer satisfaction questionnaires. These are often called 'happiness sheets' because the questions contained are so worded that the customer is obliged to give positive feedback. This type of questionnaire is worthless as an evaluation of the customer's true estimation of a product or service.

   Some organisations devise adequate questionnaires, but distribute them on a 'complete if you wish' basis, perhaps leaving them at reception counters or at service points. These questionnaires are biased towards those who feel the need to respond – usually because of dissatisfaction. Customers with grievances and grumbles are only too eager to complain, but positive feedback is seldom recorded.

However, if quality service is to be maintained and improved, it is critical that customers' perceptions be known and acted upon. Things which are going well can be developed; corrective action can be taken as a result of valid complaints. Acquiring customers is much more expensive than keeping them, and appropriate satisfaction questionnaires is one way of keeping abreast of client opinion and keeping users of your service happy.

2 Explain the purpose of the activity. Participants will devise a questionnaire to assess the satisfaction of one of their client groups. This can be an end-user of their product or service, or an internal customer (some teams serve directly other teams or departments within the organisation and have closer links with them than with external clients).

3 If necessary, divide the group into syndicate groups comprising work teams. Explain that the activity is in two parts. Firstly they should decide what principles/criteria should be used in compiling a questionnaire. When criteria have been agreed and data for inclusion has been established, they will devise the actual questions for the customer satisfaction questionnaire, recording this on flipchart paper for main group discussion.

4 Issue notepaper and pens/pencils. Allow 20 minutes for groups to compile a list of principles/criteria for compiling their questionnaire(s) and data for inclusion. You may need to give some input to start groups off (*see* Trainer notes 1).

5 In the main group, discuss the lists, adding and amending as necessary. Agreed criteria can be flipcharted.

6 Set the group(s) to work compiling the questions for their questionnaire(s). They should write these up on flipchart paper (30 minutes). They should refer to the agreed criteria, and make their questionnaires as attractive and user friendly as possible. They should consider how best to extract useful feedback from customers e.g. by succinctness; by using jargon-free language; by asking closed questions to establish facts, and open questions for clarification, and so on.

7 Reconvene main group and discuss each team's questionnaire (*see* Trainer notes 2).

8 Close the activity by establishing what participants have learned from the exercise, and how they might transfer the learning to the workplace.

TRAINER NOTES 1

The following criteria need to be considered. This is not an exclusive list; general principles apply, but details will vary depending on groups represented.

Attractive layout

Close-set, small type or a cluttered layout is immediately off–putting.

Polite approach

You are requesting a favour from your customers. Explain why you want them to fill in the questionnaire, and thank them for taking the time to complete it.

Incentive

What's in it for them? Answer: ongoing evaluation in order to maintain/improve quality of product or service.

Simplicity

Questions should be few – maximum of 12 – unambiguous and easy to understand.

Jargon free

Questions must be free of technical language, acronyms etc.

Succinctness

Questions should be carefully thought out and composed; use as few words as possible to convey meaning.

Confidentiality

Forms can be completed anonymously, or you might want to ask for the name and address of the customer – if they are prepared to give it. Whichever you choose the customer must be assured of the confidential nature of the questionnaire.

Style of question

Tick boxes save the customer time, but limit the range of possible responses, so should not be used exclusively. Avoid giving choices where customers can 'sit on the fence' e.g. *Excellent, Very good, Good, Satisfactory, Unsatisfactory*.

Where five choices are offered, most often the third / middle response will be used. If only four are used, the customer must choose a degree of negative or positive response, which gives a clearer indication of satisfaction.

Where tick boxes are used, allow enough space for the customer to give a reason for their response should they wish to do so. You could add the word 'Why?' after the boxes, indicating to the customer that you want more detail.

Focus

Concentrate your questions on the most important parts of doing business with your customers – from their point of view.

Where and how?

Don't pester customers to complete the form. Questionnaires can be left at reception or service points, can be given to customers on completion of business, at point of sale, or sent to them. If the latter, supply prepaid envelopes.

Follow up

A letter reminds the customer of your existence and shows that the questionnaires are taken seriously and acted upon.

TRAINER NOTES 2

The questions set will vary from group to group depending on their line of work and the customers, external or internal, that they have chosen to target in their questionnaires.

The following gives some indication of the type of question and the formats which could be applied.

Data collection

Name and address (optional, but useful to check contact history).

Details of product purchased or service received (if questionnaire is aimed at end-user).

Closed questions to establish facts

Were access and parking facilities adequate?

Open questions to establish facts

In what way might we improve our service to you?

Tick box, and other types of question formats

Why did you choose this organisation?

☐ Used before ☐ Recommended ☐ Reputation

☐ Advertisement ☐ Other (Please give details)

Rate how satisfied you are with the service we provide on a scale of 1–10 ☐
where 1 = very poor, and 10 = excellent.

Why? _____

Were the instructions

☐ Very helpful ☐ Helpful

☐ Misleading ☐ Not very helpful

How could they be improved? _____

On visiting the sales office did you feel your reception to be

☐ Offhand ☐ Polite ☐ Friendly ☐ Welcoming

☐ Coercive ☐ Apathetic ☐ Helpful ☐ Respectful

☐ Relaxed ☐ Hurried ☐ Efficient ☐ Aggressive

Comments: _____

_____

Activity 26

• •

PRESENTING STANDARDS

Description

This activity differs from others in the book. Rather than being an exercise in itself, it offers a method of training – an alternative to the lecture for presenting information. It gives a formula for participative learning which can be applied to any subject where the 'chalk and talk' method would normally be used.

This formula requires the trainer to have both a substantial knowledge of the subject-matter to be presented, and the preparation time to develop a questionnaire to test participants' understanding of the material. A list of suitable literature on quality systems and standards is provided (*see* Trainer notes 1). Further in-house information, or material pertinent to the sector or industry represented on the course could also be used.

Aim

Participants have the opportunity to take shared responsibility for helping each other gain an understanding of some of the major principles and concepts of a topic – in this case, quality systems and standards. Besides learning, in a participative way, about a complex topic, they will have the opportunity to practise a number of skills – listening, questioning, giving and receiving feedback, and presentation techniques.

Time

Four sessions of 1 – 2 hours

Time

- Reference materials as described below
- Notepaper, pens/pencils, flipchart paper, markers
- (Optional) Overhead transparencies (OHTs) and pens
- (Optional) Overhead projector (OHP)

Method

Trainer preparation

Decide what information you intend to distribute to participants, and what additional reference material you intend to provide. For example, if you have three or four separate articles covering different aspects of a topic, these could be used for the group teaching exercise. It might be necessary also to provide general data for all participants – giving an overall framework – plus reference material should individuals want to check details or require more in-depth information.

After completing the exercise, to reinforce learning, and to check that every participant has an adequate knowledge of the subject, a questionnaire should be devised. Details of how to organise this are given (*see* Trainer notes 2).

1 Explain that participants will work (alone, in pairs, triads, or small groups – trainer's option) and will be given written material from which to work. Each group will cover a different aspect of the same topic. The task, for the first session, is to study the data, and to begin to think about how to present the information to other group members. The second session will be devoted to planning the presentation, producing diagrams or prepared flipchart sheets/OHTs. The third session will be the presentations with questions and feedback, and the final session will consist of a questionnaire to test all participants' understanding of the material presented with an optional follow-up of how this knowledge can be related to their own work situations.

2 Session 1 Issue (pairs, triads etc.) with any general material, plus their assigned article(s). Inform group where additional reference material might be found. Ensure that there are sufficient resources in the course room. Explain that during the actual presentation, this study material may not be used, i.e. they cannot just read the article(s) to the main group. They will be teaching the others from their own understanding of the material. Personal notes can be used, of course, and participants should consider using flipchart or OHTs for visual complements to presentations. Each presentation should last 15–20 minutes.

3 Session 2 This session is devoted to refining the presentation and producing any necessary visual aids. (If groups are advanced in planning, the first presentation and feedback could be included at the end of this session.)

4 Session 3 This is potentially the longest session, depending on the total number of presentations to be covered. No more than three should be attempted if there is to be adequate time for questions and feedback.

Presentation and communication skills can be assessed against the following criteria:

- thoroughness of preparation
- inclusion of all salient points
- ideas presented clearly and simply

- explanation of technical terms
- no jargon
- logical ordering of material
- implications explained – concepts suggested
- questions invited
- checks regularly for understanding
- summarising of key points
- time management of presentation.

If questions have not been forthcoming throughout each presentation, invite the group to put questions to the presenter and partner(s) to ensure full understanding of the material. Invite comments on the presentation and give constructive feedback.

5 Session 4 Run any outstanding presentations. Issue a copy of a question-naire (*see* Trainer notes 2) to each participant. These should be completed individually.

From the results of the questionnaire, determine how much/little infor-mation participants retained. Field any questions. Discuss any concerns or outstanding misunderstandings about the topic material. (Optional) lead a short discussion about the application of the learning for individuals in the workplace.

TRAINER NOTES 1

Books

Jackson, P. and Ashton, D. (1993) *Implementing Quality Through BS5750 (ISO 9000)*, Kogan Page: London. A practical introduction to BS5750 plus an action plan for successfully meeting the requirements of the standard. It contains an overview of how to obtain BS5750, followed by full details in chapter format. Holmes, K. (1991) *Implementing BS5750*, PIRA International Leatherhead. Background to BS5750, the requirements, implementation, documentation, questions and answers.

Guides

British Standard Quality Systems available from:
BSI Quality Assurance
PO Box 375
Linford Wood
Milton Keynes MK14 6LL

Articles

'How to achieve BS5750', *Small Business Confidential* (April 1992) no. 104, pp. 4–6. How BS5750 works, the advantages of accreditation, certification bodies, use of consultants. Case studies.

Brierley, J.C., 'Achieving BS5750 registration', *Company Secretary's Review* (July 1992) vol. 16, no. 4, pp. 24–26. How assessors evaluate procedures. Consequences of a successful assessment for operating procedures in the future.

Green, G. D., 'Document control for BS5750', *Transition* (July 1992) vol. 92, no. 7. Methods by which document control requirements can be established and maintained.

TRAINER NOTES 2

How to devise a questionnaire

Study the text to identify the key knowledge points – those essential to the participants' understanding of the material. Formulate questions around these points; don't ask a question about an unimportant issue, just because it's easier to do so.

Keep to short answer questions, and link each question to an objective. Write in a direct, active way. Use crisp, concise language. Ensure your meaning is clear. Avoid 'lifting' words or phrases directly from the text, as this provides clues for answering and does not necessarily accurately assess participants' understanding.

Questions should be arranged in sequential order to parallel the text(s) used.

Types of question:

1 **True / False** statements – e.g. 'Is the following statement true or false?' Certificate holders of BS5750 may also use the ISO and EN Standards' mark.

TRUE / FALSE

If possible, give several statements, e.g. 'Tick whether each of the following statements is true or false.' True / false responses give the participant a 50/50 chance of success, so should not be used exclusively in a questionnaire.

2 **Multi-choice** questions. There should be between three and five options, and the following guidelines should be followed:

● There should be only one correct response, but alternatives should be feasible so that participants have to consider seriously all the options. Avoid trivial or implausible answers as the participant will learn nothing from the process of rejection.

● If several multi-choice questions are used, the correct options should be placed at random in the sequences.

● The options offered should be balanced in length. There is a tendency, in compilers of questionnaires, to provide more detail in the correct answers than in near-miss alternatives.

Two more tips: always record the correct answer before compiling and filling in the false options. If the alternatives are plausible enough, you may forget which answer is the correct one! If you find difficulty thinking up suitable alternatives, ask several colleagues to give you the answer to the relevant question. The chances are that some will give incorrect or incomplete responses, but their answers should be near enough to be plausible, and can be used in your questionnaire.

3 **Quiz-type** questions – e.g. 'From the following list, which procedures need to be introduced to meet BS5750 requirements for final inspection?' or 'Procedure formats need to contain a number of features. *Purpose, Scope* and *Definitions* are three; name another two.'

4 **Sequencing** questions – e.g. 'These procedures need to be followed in the registration phase, but are shown in the wrong order. List them correctly.'

There are many other more elaborate methods of compiling questions to reinforce learning. The ones suggested here call for short responses, or ticking boxes, and are the most suitable in the context of this activity.

Optional alternative

NB This depends on the ability of the participants represented, and the preparation time available.

An alternative to compiling a questionnaire before the event is to involve the participants, adding another dimension to the activity. As part of the exercise, at Step 3 issue the above guide and ask each pair / triad etc. to compose questions on their section of text to test their colleagues' understanding of the material presented. Collect, check, refine etc., and reproduce for distribution at the final session.

Activity 27

• •

STOP AND THINK

Description

This is a post-course activity, so there are no processing notes which apply to on-course facilitation. It is easy to be fired with enthusiasm during a good training event but introducing new techniques, improved systems, or change of any kind is always more demanding than talking about it. This activity is included for participants to use back at the workplace and with their work teams. It is intended for use as a review tool so that teams can stop and think about how they are handling the desired change. The activity allows for reflection on both goal achievement and team/group process.

Aim

To assist participants to reflect on the process of implementing change and to identify facets of the change management process in their own work teams.

Time

10 minutes

Resources

- Copy of the Exercise for each participant
- Further copy of the Exercise for each syndicate group

Method

1 Trainer input: to explain the activity. Participants will be issued with exercise sheets which will provide a structure which they can then use in the work situation to review how their management of change is proceeding. This structure may be used as a regular review mechanism or as an occasional snapshot. The activity embraces some of the thinking included in recent writing on change – notably Tom Peters – which sees change as a constant. The most successful organisations/teams, according to such writers, are those which recognise this paradox and function accordingly.

2 Issue the Exercise. Allow time for reading and take any questions. Allow 10 minutes for this.

Questions you might use:

- Are people clear on how to use the document in the workplace?
- How much time should be set aside for it to be used effectively?
- Should it be used regularly or occasionally?
- What preconditions might there be for the document to work most effectively?
- If a group or team feels they score low on some of the issues, what could they do about it?
- How useful do people feel the document will be in practice?

3 Close the activity.

EXERCISE

REVIEWING THE PROCESS OF CHANGE MANAGEMENT

With your team, allow a few moments for each team member to complete the form individually. Then come together and complete a 'group consensus sheet'. You can think of the document as an agenda with items designed to provoke discussion.

Rate each item on the scale shown.

Task processes in our team

T1: Goals and targets Involving change

LOW SCORE   1   2   3   4   5   6   HIGH SCORE

Our goals and targets are unclear, or are confused, or conflicting, or too many / diverse, or unrealistic. There is little commitment to achieving the goals and targets. Our routine work gets in the way of change and innovation tasks.	Our goals and targets are clear. The perception by all is clear. There is commitment to achieving the goals and targets. We balance our routine and our innovative / change tasks.

T2: Progress monitoring

LOW SCORE   1   2   3   4   5   6   HIGH SCORE

Progress towards our goals and targets is not measured or carried out regularly. Perceptions of progress differ across the team. There is no interest in taking an overview of progress.	We have regular and effective progress reviews. Perceptions of progress are shared. There is an overall shared concern about progress towards the overall goal.

T3: Decision-making

LOW SCORE   1   2   3   4   5   6   HIGH SCORE

Essential decisions don't get made. Responsibility for decision-making is unclear. Decisions made by some team members do not gain full commitment of rest of team.	Consensus is sought and gained. Decision-making responsibility is clear and understood by all. Decisions made are fully supported.

T4: The environment

LOW SCORE   1   2   3   4   5   6   HIGH SCORE

We function in isolation. We could be accused of living in an ivory tower. We don't have mechanisms for testing how our changes are being received by others outside our team. We don't know what our customers want. We have to struggle to get relevant information.

We have well-developed listening and testing mechanisms for how our changes are affecting / will affect others outside our team. We are conscious of the impact of external reality on our thinking and decision-making. We are acutely aware of what our customers want. Our information base is well developed and accessible.

Team process in our team

P1: Participation

LOW SCORE   1   2   3   4   5   6   HIGH SCORE

There are dominant and passive people in our team. Some are ignored. Some are valued less than others. There is a lot of cross-talking and interruption.

All people are heard. All opinions are valued.

P2: Feelings

LOW SCORE   1   2   3   4   5   6   HIGH SCORE

Suppressed or frowned on. Discomfort with expression of feelings. If expressed then ignored or cause embarrassment.

Freely expressed. Encouraged. Supportive handling of feelings. Seen as important indicators.

P3: Group problems

LOW SCORE   1   2   3   4   5   6   HIGH SCORE

Avoided. Not faced up to. Remedies discussed rather than underlying causes.

Diagnosis of group problems. Solutions tackle basic rather than presenting problems.

P4: Leadership

LOW SCORE   1   2   3   4   5   6   HIGH SCORE

Team leadership needs not met or leader(s) dominate inappropriately. Team strengths not recognised.

Leadership style is appropriate to team's needs. Adaptable to changing needs.

P5: Trust

LOW SCORE   1   2   3   4   5   6   HIGH SCORE

High level of distrust. Team interaction characterised by polite, guarded, careful responses. Listening is at a superficial level. Fear of criticising or be criticised. Back-stabbing or formation of informal cliques and alliances.

High level of trust. Open sharing of concerns and ideas. Responses from the team are actively welcomed and acted on. Negativity can be expressed without fear of reprisals. No need for informal cliques or alliances.

P6: Creativity and team growth

LOW SCORE   1   2   3   4   5   6   HIGH SCORE

Low creativity. No original thinking or any that surfaces is quickly squashed or seen as a threat. Fear of innovation or challenging established order. Discomfort with change. Routine is the order of the day. People stereotyped in their roles.

High creativity. Open minds to new ideas and ways of thinking. Support for people's needs to develop and try new things. Change is seen as opportunity. People are adaptable and the team overall is flexible.

6 The learning event

Activity 28

· ·

IN THE MOOD

Description

This is a selection of five short activities which can be used at the beginning of a training session to set the mood. Ice-breakers are an important part of any training event – even if participants already know each other – in that they focus participants' minds on the training to come.

Aim

To create a learning environment which encourages participation, involvement and co-operation.

A: Customer care

This activity is designed to quickly focus participants' minds on what customer care entails.

Time

30 minutes

Resources

- Notepaper, pens/pencils
- Flipchart and marker pen for trainer use

Method

A1 Divide group into pairs/triads. Issue notepaper and pens/pencils if required.

A2 Instruct participants to write the letters which make up the word C–U–S–T–O–M–E–R vertically down the left-hand side of the page.

A3 They have 15 minutes to think of words or phrases, beginning with each of the initial letters, which have connections or associations with customer care.

A4 In the main group, ask pairs/triads to call out their chosen words, giving a brief explanation of the relevance to customer care. Record these words on flipchart paper (*see* Trainer notes). It doesn't matter if groups haven't been able to think of words or phrases for every letter; the important thing is that they have concentrated their thinking on customer care issues.

A5 Close the activity.

A: TRAINER NOTES

Below are some examples of words and phrases which could have relevance to the concept of customer care.

C Care, client, confidence, concern, consideration, consumer.

U User friendly, up-market, uppermost.

S Satisfaction, service, standards, solicitude, success.

T TQM (Total Quality Management), tact, thoughtfulness.

O Obliging, observant, ongoing, opinions, opportunity.

M Measurable, motivation, matchless, merit, monitor.

E Effort, ethics, explanations, exemplary, effectiveness.

R Reliability, responsible, reputation, recognition, review.

You may have participants who include phrases such as C an't be bothered with it; U tter waste of time; S tressful; T ranquillisers needed – and so on. These (hopefully flippant) responses are still useful discussion points.

B: Problem-solving

The following exercises test problem-solving through logical or lateral thinking.

Time

30 minutes

Resources

- Copy of Exercise for each participant

Method

B1 Participants work in pairs to solve the five problems (15 minutes). If anyone has encountered one of the puzzles before, and knows the answer, they should allow others to find the solution without spoiling the fun!

B2 In the main group, discuss solutions offered. The first three require logical thinking; the other two are lateral thinking puzzles.

B3 Close the activity by observing that problems may not always be solved by pursuing logical, or vertical, thinking. Often, by using lateral thinking – turning the problem on its head – new ideas emerge which can be added to the list of possible solutions for consideration.

B: EXERCISE

You have 15 minutes to solve the following puzzles.

1 Joan, Margaret and Vera own a small dinghy which they need to row from the mainland to their island cottage each day. The dinghy is small – and Vera is large! It can hold either Vera, or both the smaller women at any one time; it would sink under the weight of all three. How can they all get to the island in as few trips as possible?

2 A tramp can make a whole cigarette out of every 5 cigarette butts he finds. How many cigarettes can he make from 25 butts?

3 Tom, Dick and Harry are neighbours. They live in three, adjoining houses. One is a librarian, one is a teacher, and one is a barrister (though not in that order). Dick lives in the middle house. The teacher looks after Harry's cat when he's away. Tom is a heavy sleeper, so the librarian knocks on Tom's wall at 8.00 a.m. on weekdays to make sure he gets up on time. What is each man's profession?

4 John and Jack are playing the last hole in a game of golf. John drives off the tee. It is a splendid shot; the ball drops just short of the green, but to his dismay, rolls into a paper bag which some unthinking person has dropped. If he removes the ball from the bag it will cost him a penalty shot, but if he tries to hit ball and bag together it will spoil his shot, and there is no guarantee that ball and bag will part company. Nevertheless he makes a birdie and wins the game. How did he solve the problem?

5 A father and his son are involved in a traffic accident. The father is killed out-right, but the son survives although he has dreadful injuries. The hospital to which he is taken decide that the son shouldn't be moved, but that the country's leading brain surgeon should be called for. On seeing the boy the surgeon exclaims, 'Oh my God, that's my son!' That is so, but the surgeon is not the boy's father. Explain.

B: TRAINER NOTES

Solutions

1 Three trips. Trip 1 – the two lighter women row across and leave one on the island; the second rows back to the mainland and gets out of the boat. Trip 2 – Vera rows across to the island alone; gets out of the boat. The woman left on the island originally, rows the boat back to the mainland to collect the second lighter woman. Trip 3 – both lighter women row to the island.

2 Six cigarettes. He makes a cigarette out of five butts – that's five cigarettes in all. If he smokes these cigarettes, they produce another five butts from which he can make a sixth cigarette.

3 Tom is the teacher; Dick is the librarian; Harry is the barrister. The teacher must be either Tom or Dick (looks after Harry's cat). The librarian must be Harry or Dick (knocks on Tom's wall). The barrister, therefore, must be either Tom or Harry. Because Dick lives in the middle house, it would be impossible for Tom to knock on Harry's wall or vice versa, so the librarian must be Dick. Options for the teacher were Tom or Dick. Having established Dick's profession, the teacher must be Tom and thus the barrister must be Harry.

4 A possible solution: John set light to the paper bag. When it was reduced to ashes, and the ball exposed, he played the shot and made a birdie. Here the problem was turned on its head and lateral thinking was used. Unable to see a way of getting the ball from the paper bag, the golfer solved the problem by getting the bag away from the ball.

5 The surgeon was the boy's mother. This is a typical example of how stereotyping and preconceived ideas can get in the way of effective problem-solving.

C: Teams

The most effective teams care about team and organisational objectives, but also about individuals' needs and interests. This activity discovers how much team members know about their work colleagues – as people.

Time

30 minutes

Resources

● Enough copies of the Exercise for every participant to have a copy for each member of her or his work team.

Method

C1 If necessary, divide group into their work teams. Issue each participant with the exercise – one for every member of their team.

C2 Participants will complete a form for each member of her or his team (10–15 minutes). If unsure of any response, leave it blank – or better still, guess! Participants will then discuss all the forms within their teams, individuals adding or clarifying information about themselves (15 minutes). Explain that the exercise is light-hearted. It is intended to firm relationships by knowing each other better. However, assure all participants that they need only share what they want to share with their team colleagues.

C3 Close the activity.

C: EXERCISE

NAME OF COLLEAGUE _____

NICKNAME _____
_____

PARTNER'S NAME _____
_____

PARTNER'S NICKNAME _____
_____

CHILDREN'S NAMES AND AGES _____
_____

WHAT PETS? THEIR NAMES? _____
_____

WHERE SPENT HOLIDAY LAST YEAR _____
_____

WHERE SPENDING HOLIDAY THIS YEAR _____
_____

HOBBIES _____
_____

FAVOURITE SPORT _____
_____

PLAYED OR SUPPORTED? _____
_____

FAVOURITE TV VIEWING _____
_____

FAVOURITE FOOD _____
_____

HOW PREFERS TO SPEND LEISURE TIME _____
_____

D: Brainstorming

If performed correctly, brainstorming is a way of including all members of a team, in a non-threatening way, thus producing the maximum number of creative ideas/possible solutions to problems. All suggestions, however inappropriate they might at first seem, should be recorded unchallenged. When ideas have been exhausted, suggestions can be examined, clarified, amended, accepted or rejected. *Reverse brainstorming* can also take place – looking at the possibilities and brainstorming all the problems associated with the ideas. This helps give an objective view of ideas or solutions.

   This activity should be used to demonstrate the dynamics of brainstorming, but should not be taken too seriously!

Time

30 minutes

Resources

● Flipchart and marker pen for trainer use

Method

D1 Write up the topic 'Dog Fouling' on a sheet of flipchart paper. Instruct participants to call out their ideas on how to deal with this problem. Every suggestion, however daft or obscure, should be recorded. Everyone should be encouraged to contribute. Do not comment; merely record.

D2 When ideas have been exhausted, consider the list. Often, it is one of the most apparently silly ideas that points the way to a solution.

D3 Close the activity by emphasising the value of brainstorming to teamwork. Brainstorming:

   ● involves everyone
   ● focuses the mind
   ● encourages creativity
   ● meets individual's needs for team inclusion
   ● encourages communication – listening, information sharing etc.
   ● maximises ideas/possible solutions to problems
   ● minimises risk of overlooking elements of the problem or issue under question.

E: Intelligence test

This is a general, 'getting into learning mode' activity, and is more competitive and less individually threatening if the group is divided into pairs or small syndicate groups.

Time

30 minutes

Resources

- Copy of the Exercise for each participant
- (Optional) Small prize – chocolate bar? – for winners

Method

E1 Divide the group into pairs or syndicate groups. Issue a copy of the Exercise to each participant. Explain that some problems have logical solutions; others require creativity. Don't take the exercise too seriously! (Optional) there will be a small prize for the winning pair or group. Set them to work (15 minutes, or the first to finish).

E2 Go through each question (*see* Trainer notes) discussing answers, reasoning, the approach used and so on. Allocate marks according to correct answers/ingenious solutions. Trainer's decision final! Announce the winning pair or group.

E3 Close the activity by observing that some of the problems posed can be solved logically; others have several equally valid solutions and involve creativity. Some can be solved individually; others might benefit from a team approach. The main object of the exercise was to concentrate the mind away from the 9–5 routine and what might be happening at the workplace, and focus it on learning and the training to come.

 **E: EXERCISE**

Write your answers on this sheet.

1 For the purpose of this puzzle, + means divide, ÷ means multiply, – means add, and × means subtract.

36 + 6 = _____   49 – 32 = _____   12 ÷ 9 = _____   49 + 7 = _____

51 × 3 = _____   7 ÷ 6 = _____   26 × 13 = _____   8 – 6 = _____

31 – 11 = _____   96 + 12 = _____   3 ÷ 9 = _____   25 × 18 = _____

2 Underline the odd one out:

CUSTOMER – crust, rote, muse, trim, curse, store.

3 Create a witty definition for each of the following:
Example: TURNOVER – Move on to side to stop snoring

SERVICE _____

DISCUSS _____

FEEDBACK _____

CONTACT _____

SECURE _____

ORGANISE _____

4 Insert the missing numbers

(a) 36 30 24 18 _____   (b) 12 25 52 107 _____

(c) 126 (300) 201   (d) 2   4   6   8   ____ ____ ____ ____
    354 (   ) 376

5 Correct the following:

(a) Each type have different qualities.

(b) 'Here's the receipts for your order.'

(c) 'Don't never do that again!'

(d) Of the two samples, this is the best.

(e) We have a committment to quality

(f) Our trainer resides at 2 Acacia Avenue.

E: TRAINER NOTES

Answers

1 $36 + 6 = \underline{6}$ $49 - 32 = \underline{81}$ $12 \div 9 = \underline{108}$ $49 + 7 = \underline{7}$

    $51 \times 3 = \underline{48}$ $7 \div 6 = \underline{42}$ $26 \times 13 = \underline{13}$ $8 - 6 = \underline{14}$

    $31 - 11 = \underline{42}$ $96 + 12 = \underline{8}$ $3 \div 9 = \underline{27}$ $25 \times 18 = \underline{7}$

2 Trim. The other words comprise letters found in CUSTOMER.

3 SERVICE – depraved baronet

    DISCUSS – athlete's saucer

    FEEDBACK – regurgitate

    CONTACT – diplomatic swindler

    SECURE – bishop's panacea

    ORGANISE – the piped instruments have it!

4 (a) 12 – the numbers are reduced by 6 each time

    (b) 218 – the numbers are doubled, plus 1; doubled plus two and so on

    (c) 88 – the difference between the two figures outside the brackets, multiplied by 4

    (d) Who-do-we-appreciate (or you could have 10, 12, 14, 16)

5 (a) Each type <u>has</u> . . . (singular)

    (b) 'Here <u>are</u> receipts . . . (plural)

    (c) 'Don't <u>ever</u> . . . (double negative)

    (d) . . . this is the <u>better.</u>

    (e) Commitment (common spelling error)

    (f) WRONG. Well, you don't live at that address do you?

If participants think that one or two questions are unfair – like the last elements in 4 and 5 – explain that what is logical to one person can appear nonsense to another. The lesson to be learned is that if we get fixed in a set way of thinking, this can restrict our problem-solving ability.

Activity 29

• •
TELL IT OR SELL IT?

Description

This activity is often used in the professional development of trainers but it is equally useful to anyone who needs to take on any kind of training role, either temporary (as described in the introduction to this book) or more permanent. **In order for the activity to have validity, participants will need to have had SOME experience in a training role, however low key.** As a minimum, participants will need to have trained small groups (3 or more). 'On-the-job' training is acceptable – it is not necessary to have conducted sophisticated training courses. What matters is that participants can draw on past experience of working with trainees as a group in some kind of learning situation. Without such experience, the questionnaire at the heart of this activity will not make sense.

Aim

To make participants aware of their own training 'style', actual or potential, and to consider how this might impact on their effectiveness as trainers.

Time

1 hour

Resources

- Flipchart and marker pen for trainer use
- Copy of Exercise – Sheet A for each participant
- Copy of Exercise – Sheet B for each participant
- Copy of Handout for each participant

Method

1 Trainer input: to introduce the activity, which is designed to help people learn something of their own style as trainers (actual or potential). The results will assist participants to consider the implications of this style in developing a profile of effective trainer skills. It is wise to stress that the questionnaire is not a psychometric or psychological test; it is purely about preferences and there are no right or wrong answers.

2 Issue Exercise – Sheet A to each participant. Ask them to spend a little time working individually, completing the questionnaire. Allow 10 minutes for this. If preferred, you could distribute the questionnaire before the course and ask people to bring the completed version with them.

3 When everyone has completed their questionnaire, hand out Exercise – Sheet B and ask them to complete and add up their marks. Check people understand how to do this, offering help if necessary.

4 Issue the Handout. Allow time for participants to read it and clarify where necessary. Stress that the styles are not value-laden; no one style is necessarily better or worse than another.

5 Run a brief group discussion getting reactions to the four styles. Allow 15 minutes for this.

Questions you might use:

- Do people recognise themselves?
- Do people recognise others who they may have been trained or managed by?
- What examples can people give of the style in action?

6 Finally, run a group discussion which attempts to answer the questions (which you could usefully flipchart)*'If I have a preference which I tend to use naturally, how valid is it in all circumstances?'* and *'If I can see arguments for other styles, how can I learn different techniques and behaviours which might improve the range of styles I can draw on?'* Allow 20 minutes for this.

Questions you might use:

- Is any one style mutually exclusive of others?
- How comfortable do people feel about recognising and adopting other styles from their own preference? How do such feelings relate to scores from the exercise (i.e. the lower the score – does this mean the greater the degree of discomfort in adopting that style)?
- Can we think of examples where each of the four styles might be more appropriate than any of the others e.g. a Teacher style could be the most useful one in getting across a mathematical principle to a large group?
- Do all trainees or learners respond to the same style?
- How can people set about acquiring and practising new styles?
- To what extent are the styles based upon skills as opposed to personality and to what extent might further training enhance confidence in practising/adopting other styles?

7 Close the activity.

EXERCISE SHEET A

Training styles questionnaire

This exercise is to do with personal preferences and, as such, there are no right or wrong answers. Read through each statement and tick those with which you feel you can identify most comfortably when you are in a training role, whether training others on a course or training people 'on-the-job'. Put a cross against any which you feel least comfortable with, or would, you feel, give you the most difficulty. Leave blank those about which you have no strong feelings either way.

	When training others I feel comfortable when I...	Tick, cross or leave blank	
1	encourage learners to express their personal needs freely		1
2	am controlling the learning experience		2
3	enable learners to become more familiar with terms and rules, and understand their implications		3
4	enable learners to evaluate their own progress		4
5	give clear directions for procedures to be followed		5
6	ensure that everyone is heard		6
7	separate myself from learners and observe		7
8	involve learners in activities		8
9	encourage experimentation / practical application		9
10	share ideas rather than feelings		10
11	prepare notes and outlines		11
12	am able to show awareness of the needs of individual group members		12
13	acknowledge others' interpretations as well as my own		13
14	facilitate peer group learning		14
15	can read and respond to non-verbal behaviour		15

16	appear self-confident		16
17	enable learners to talk more than I do		17
18	feel I am well organised		18
19	operate from a theoretical base		19
20	use resources within the group		20
21	am able to evaluate performance using objective criteria		21
22	enable learners to take responsibility for / control over their learning		22
23	encourage generalisations when appropriate		23
24	draw out learners' experience – what they already know		24
25	encourage active experimentation		25
26	listen for thoughts rather than emotions		26
27	use lectures		27
28	expose own emotions and experiences		28
29	stick to the published agenda		29
30	deal with all types of expression		30
31	concentrate on one item at a time		31
32	enable learners to understand facts and terminology		32
33	act as facilitator to make experience more meaningful		33
34	am flexible / go with the flow		34
35	use hypothetical case studies and theory		35
36	use activities, projects and problems based on real life		36
37	encourage active participation		37
38	encourage learners to think independently		38
39	develop contingency plans		39
40	appear relaxed and unhurried		40

EXERCISE SHEET B

Scoring sheet for the questionnaire

In the unshaded boxes in the grid below record your scores as follows:

Score 0 for each cross   Score 2 for each blank   Score 4 for each tick

Q	L	T	P	C		Q	L	T	P	C
1						21				
2						22				
3						23				
4						24				
5						25				
6						26				
7						27				
8						28				
9						29				
10						30				
11						31				
12						32				
13						33				
14						34				
15						35				
16						36				
17						37				
18						38				
19						39				
20						40				
				←——— TOTALS ———→					

Now add the two **L** totals together: **TOTAL L SCORE** _____

Now add the two **T** totals together: **TOTAL T SCORE** _____

Now add the two **P** totals together: **TOTAL P SCORE** _____

Now add the two **C** totals together: **TOTAL C SCORE** _____

HANDOUT – TRAINER STYLES

Listener

A high scorer is comfortable with expression of personal needs and feelings in training or other situations of uncertainty. Usually flexible and able to adapt plans and programmes to ensure people can make their own contribution.

Teacher

A high scorer likes to be well organised and keep to an agreed timetable. Prefers situations where objective criteria can be used to evaluate. Tends to control learning so that time limits are observed and items are covered systematically. Probably favours a lecture style based on the 'I am the expert' perspective.

Processor

A high scorer will enjoy processing and interpreting facts, concepts, rules. May tend to be more comfortable with ideas, theories and concepts than with feelings. May prefer to use hypothetical situations as a way of discussing issues and problems 'in the abstract'.

Coach

A high scorer will prefer to involve people in learning through activity and will encourage experiential learning based on experimentation and practical applications. A coach recognises and values the contribution to overall learning that a group resource can be, especially in terms of helping people articulate their ideas and developing awareness.

Activity 30

CONSEQUENCES

Description

A course closure activity to help participants recognise the learning which has taken place, and to take responsibility to act on it. It is also a useful source of information, for the trainer, about the course's effectiveness.

Aim

To identify learning which has taken place and what changes (personal/inter-personal/corporate) need to be made.

Time

30 minutes – 1 hour

Resources

- Copy of Exercise for each participant
- Pen/pencil for each participant
- Table/desk space or clipboard on which to rest paper
- Means of attaching papers to wall

Method

1 Trainer input: to explain that participants will each receive a preprinted sheet of A4 containing a number of statements which require simple, truthful responses. They will have 15 minutes to complete these forms, after which time they will be asked to pin their statement sheets to a wall so that the trainer, and everyone in the group can go and evaluate the learning that has taken place for individuals during the course of the training programme. It would be helpful if participants feel able to identify their sheets, but anonymity should be an option for individuals.

2 Issue a copy of the Exercise to each participant. Explain that by giving this exercise a little time and thought, the completion of the statements contained can offer individuals invaluable insight, and will also help the trainer to evaluate the effectiveness of the training programme which has just been presented.

3 Let participants complete their forms. Allow participants 15 minutes for this. Depending on the content of preceding sessions, some statements may have little relevance. Participants should respond to as many as possible. After 15 minutes, or when everyone has completed their forms to their own satisfaction, ask participants to attach their sheet to a wall where everyone can see it.

4 Suggest that participants take their time to read the various sheets, to check the range of responses, and where similarities or differences occur. It is especially useful for the trainer to take time over this part of the exercise in order to maximise the effectiveness of the following discussion and course evaluation.

5 After about 15 minutes, or when everyone has had a chance to read all contributions, reassemble group for a plenary discussion. First, ask for general comments.

Questions you might use:

• Were you surprised at the similarities/differences?

• Why do you think people's reactions were so similar/different?

• Did reading others' comments give you cause to reconsider some of your responses?

This sort of questioning eventually leads to a more detailed analysis of some of the key issues for participants. In turn, this gives the trainer useful information about the course – what went well, what needs adjustment, what needed more time spent on it and so on.

6 If not already covered at Step 5, lead a short discussion on course evaluation.

Questions you might use:

• What was the most useful part of the course?

• How could it be improved?

• How could the session on .... be enhanced?

• Most of you found difficulty with .... Why was this?

7 Thank participants for their honesty and constructive support.
Close the activity.

EXERCISE – COURSE REVIEW

NAME (optional) _____

Please complete as many as are relevant, of the following statements:

I learned _____

_____

My views on / methods of _____

_____ were reinforced.

My views on _____

_____ have not altered.

I discovered that I _____

_____

I was disappointed that _____

_____

I intend to make the following personal change. _____

_____

I intend to improve my interpersonal relationship(s) by _____

_____

At work, I will endeavour to change _____

_____

Bibliography

For those who would like to read more on the theoretical background behind this book, we suggest the following, which is a very small, but representative, sample of readily available publications on training and facilitation. We have not necessarily drawn directly on all of these in our writing here, but they do offer a good coverage of relevant theory and practice. We commend them to you if you feel their titles will add to your own knowledge of this fascinating field.

Belbin, R. M., (1986) *Management teams: Why They Succeed or Fail*, Heinemann: London.

Brookfield, S. D., (1986) *Understanding and Facilitating Adult Learning*, Open University Press: Milton Keynes.

Cowling, A. G., Stanworth, M. J. K., Bennett, R. D., Curran J. and Lyons, P. (1988) *Behavioural Sciences for Managers*, Edward Arnold: London.

Harrison, R., (1990) *Training and Development*, Institute of Personnel Management: London.

Johnson, D. W. and Johnson, F. P., (1976) *Joining Together – Group Theory and Group Skills*, Prentice Hall: Eaglewood Cliffs, NJ, USA.

Kenney, J. and Reid, M. (1988) *Training Interventions*, Institute of Personnel Management: London.

Knowles, M. (1980) *The Modern Practice of Adult Education*, Cambridge Book Company: Cambridge.

Newby, A., (1992) *How to Design and Deliver Quality Service Training*, Kogan Page: London.

Peters, T., (1989) *Thriving on Chaos – Handbook for a Management Revolution*, Pan Books: London.

Peters, T. and Waterman, R. H., (1982) *In Search of Excellence*, Harper & Row: London.

Phillips, K. and Fraser, A. (1985) *The Management of Interpersonal Skills Training*, Gower: Aldershot.

Stewart, J. (1991) *Managing Change Through Training and Development*, Kogan Page: London.

Tight, M. (ed.) (1987) *Adult Learning and Education*, Croom Helm: Beckenham.

Weightman, J., (1990) *Managing Human Resources*, Institute of Personnel Management: London.